Career Launcher

Law

Career Launcher series

Advertising and Public Relations
Computers and Programming
Education
Energy
Fashion
Film
Finance
Food Services
Hospitality
Internet
Health Care Management
Health Care Providers
Law
Law Enforcement and Public Safety
Manufacturing
Nonprofit Organizations
Performing Arts
Professional Sports Organizations
Real Estate
Recording Industry
Television
Video Games

Career Launcher

Law

Amy Hackney Blackwell

Ferguson Publishing
An imprint of Infobase Publishing

Career Launcher: **Law**

Copyright © 2010 by Infobase Publishing, Inc.

Ferguson
An imprint of Infobase Publishing
132 West 31st Street
New York NY 10001

Library of Congress Cataloging-in-Publication Data

Hackney Blackwell, Amy.
    Law / by Amy Hackney Blackwell.
      p. cm. — (Career launcher)
    Includes bibliographical references and index.
    ISBN-13: 978-0-8160-7970-4 (hardcover : alk. paper)
    ISBN-10: 0-8160-7970-6 (hardcover : alk. paper)
  1. Law—Vocational guidance—United States—Juvenile literature. I. Title.
    KF297.H27 2009
    340.023'73—dc22

                                    2009021394

Ferguson books are available at special discounts when purchased in bulk quantities for businesses, associations, institutions, or sales promotions. Please call our Special Sales Department in New York at (212) 967-8800 or (800) 322-8755.

You can find Ferguson on the World Wide Web at http://www.fergpubco.com

Produced by Print Matters, Inc.
Text design by A Good Thing, Inc.
Cover design by Takeshi Takahashi
Cover printed by Art Print, Taylor, PA
Book printed and bound by Maple Press, York, PA
Date printed: June 2010

Printed in the United States of America

10 9 8 7 6 5 4 3 2 1

This book is printed on acid-free paper.

Contents

Foreword

If you are reading this book you are probably considering work in the legal field. That's great. I have been a lawyer for over 27 years and I am still excited by what I do.

I hold a senior executive position in the U.S. Department of Treasury, that of division counsel/associate chief counsel in the Office of Chief Counsel for the Internal Revenue Service. My office is essentially the law firm serving the Internal Revenue Service in its administration of the tax law as it applies to exempt organizations; retirement plans; federal, state, local, and Indian tribal governments; and as it applies to all taxpayers in the areas of executive compensation, health and welfare benefits, employment tax, and other related areas of tax law. Our legal office comprises about 150 people in Washington and seven other major cities. These attorneys, paralegals, and other support personnel work on legislation, publish tax regulations and other guidance, and litigate on behalf of the United States in the areas of law under our jurisdiction.

I should confess that being a lawyer was not my original plan. My parents trained me to be a pianist and I focused my college courses around my desire to become an animal behaviorist. Reality demanded that I get a paying job and I did, earning enough to support myself and enjoy a share in a beach cottage from May through October. One evening I sat and talked with friends on that beach, realizing that they were moving on in their careers and that I was uninterested in moving forward in what I was doing. When I expressed my feelings of restlessness and frustration a friend laughed and said you love wrestling every idea and inquiry to the ground and then persuading us of the answer; you should become a lawyer. Without any certainty that this would be right for me I decided to try it, took the LSATs, and enrolled in the evening law program at Suffolk University School of Law in Boston.

Three weeks later I had no time for the beach, barely time for laundry, and realized I had found what I wanted to do with my life. When I shared this excitement with a senior executive in my office he said quietly, "I can see you love the study of law, I wonder if you will love the practice." If you are considering a career in the legal field you will spend a significant part of your life in that endeavor. The question he asked me is a key question for you in making your choice and it is a question I think this book can help you answer.

Legal jobs by their nature are not easy. The law itself is both complex and constantly evolving. Thus the jobs in it require expertise and constant learning. Further the issues entrusted to you usually matter deeply to the parties affected and often to the community at large. It is through law that society seeks justice and the prevention of injustice. Thus those working in the field carry a particular duty to society to both seek and speak the truth. For example the duty of the prosecution, under the guidelines of the American Bar Association, is to "seek justice not merely convict." As a practical example in my present position at Treasury, as when I litigated on behalf of the United States as an attorney with the United States Department of Justice, this standard means that I should not bring a case because I could win it. Rather I should only bring it because I should win it; because that is the right outcome for the people of the United States. Similarly in litigation defense counsel is charged both with providing excellent representation on behalf of the client and with serving as an officer of the court responsible for proceeding with integrity.

Thus the bottom line is that while jobs in the legal arena can be richly rewarding they are also difficult, demanding, and not easily left behind when you leave work for the day. I would, therefore, quibble with the young lawyer in the movie *Legally Blonde* who blithely quoted Aristotle as saying "the law is reason, free from passion." Instead, for those of you considering working in this field I would say that to be happy and successful in this endeavor you must be passionate about the importance of your work while keeping that passion from biasing your analysis. I can now answer the question that long ago executive asked and say, yes, I love the practice of law as well. Not in every detail, the long hours can be draining, the enormous importance of ascertaining all relevant facts and law tedious, the moments when adversarial practice becomes too heated frustrating, but these challenges are outweighed by the excitement of crafting solutions and advancing overall equity.

In general, in considering whether you are suited to this field I would suggest asking yourself these questions: Do you have great skill in written and oral communication? Do you find joy in reasoned debate? Do you love problem solving and negotiation? Do you have a love of research and discovery combined with an ability to master the detail you unearth? And do you feel a strong abiding commitment to justice and equity? If so I encourage you heartily to consider becoming a member of the legal community, whether as a lawyer, paralegal, researcher, or technical consultant. I promise you that while there will be frustrations, the joys will greatly outweigh them.

—Nancy J. Marks
Division counsel, U.S. Department of Treasury
Washington, D.C.

Acknowledgments

Many thanks to Ryan, Philip, Frank, Uncle Frank, Laura, David, and especially Nancy for their help and hard work, all of it non-billable.

Introduction

There are many approaches to finding fulfillment in a legal career. For each person, the best route turns on who you are and what you want to do. Maybe you want to be a lawyer. Maybe you would rather start working sooner, so you would prefer to be a paralegal or perhaps a legal secretary. Perhaps you are a paralegal or attorney interested in moving into one of the niches now appearing in the legal field, such as litigation technology. Whichever your preference, this book can help.

Why So Much Emphasis on Attorneys?

Most of this book focuses on what lawyers do. That is not intended as a slight to other legal jobs. The fact is, though, the legal profession actually has one main job: lawyer, or attorney. Every other job within the field exists to help lawyers do their work. Other legal professions are quite new, too; up until the 1970s, paralegals didn't even exist as such, and the only legal staff members were secretaries.

With a few exceptions, paralegals can and do perform the exact same tasks that lawyers do. The other jobs you will find listed in the chapter "On the Job" are similar; they exist to further the work of attorneys, which in many cases means doing the work of attorneys.

Of course, attorneys must supervise the work of their employees, so any work that is submitted to a court or a client must be approved by a lawyer before it goes out the door. Attorneys have more training in the law than paralegals and other staffers, and they must all pass an examination to prove that they know their stuff. That is why for the most part attorneys make the highest salaries of those who work in the legal field. (That's not true across the board; check out "State of the Industry" to see how attorney and paralegal salaries compare.)

How to Use This Book

This book is meant to help you make decisions about a legal career and then to help you go about pursuing success whether you are starting from scratch or already working in the legal field. The chapter "Industry History" describes the development of the legal profession from the beginning of human history until the present day.

The law has been around for a very long time; historians have found numerous legal documents that are nearly 4,000 years old. The lengthy history has made the law into what it is today. Law in the United States combines elements of ancient Greek and Roman law, Germanic and Celtic law, the English common law, and the Napoleonic code, along with a smattering of traditions from Spain and ideas from Enlightenment philosophers. That diverse background explains why every state has its own legal system, why every state governs its own legal profession, and why every lawyer must also study federal law.

The chapter entitled "State of the Industry" contains statistics on the number of attorneys and paralegals in the United States, salary information, and prospects for growth. It also discusses conventions such as the billable hour, the organization of the legal profession into state bars, and the way technology is changing the practice of law.

Turn to "On the Job" to find out exactly what jobs exist within the legal field. There are basically two main jobs: attorney and legal assistant, which can include secretaries and paralegals. But those jobs are distributed throughout an extremely varied profession. If you go into the legal field, you will have to choose between private and government practice. If you go into private practice, you will have to decide between working in a law firm or as in-house counsel in a corporation. You will have to decide whether you are primarily a litigator or a transactional lawyer. And you will have to decide which specialties are yours; gone are the days of jack-of-all trade attorneys who did a little of everything. Today attorneys and their paralegals specialize in one or two areas.

"Tips for Success" will tell you how to become a lawyer or paralegal, how to ace your interviews, and how to succeed once you have a job. Becoming a lawyer is time-consuming and expensive. Before you begin, you really ought to think about all that is involved: taking the LSAT, choosing a school, excelling as a student, and finding jobs and clerkships. The most successful law students have considered all these problems before they even begin applying to schools. If you would rather be a paralegal or secretary, your path to work will be shorter, but you will still have to work hard and be competent in order to succeed.

The legal field has its own language. Look to "Talk Like a Pro" to learn some of the jargon that you will have to know as a legal professional. Finally, "Resources" lists a number of Web sites and books that can help you on your way to a successful legal career.

Chapter 1

Industry History

Laws have been part of human society for a very long time. And where there are laws, there have invariably been lawyers and judges. The legal profession got its start in ancient Babylon and the Near East and has continued unbroken to the present day.

Law in the Ancient World

Any time people live close together and share resources, they run into disagreements. When ancient people started living in towns and cities, they quickly discovered this fact. They had to decide how to allocate their water, how to organize their agriculture, and how to handle family problems. Laws were the answer. Historians know of laws dating from nearly 4,000 years ago in ancient Babylon and the Near East. These laws influenced the laws of later societies in Greece and Rome, which in turn have become the basis for laws we have today.

Babylon: the Code of Hammurabi

Some of the earliest known laws date from around 1760 b.c.e., when a king of Babylon called Hammurabi united several kingdoms into the Babylonian Empire. Babylon was in Mesopotamia, the region between the Tigris and Euphrates Rivers in what is now Iraq. The Babylonian empire consisted of several city-states. All of these city-states created laws to help organize society in crowded cities with limited access to water. Archaeologists have found thousands of documents from that period that provide a vivid picture of law in ancient Mesopotamia. Contracts, receipts, accounts, deeds, written decisions by judges, private letters, and many other writings exist to show that the people of this early civilization were surrounded by law.

Hammurabi is famous today for his collection of laws, or code. The Code of Hammurabi is the best-preserved of the laws from this period and has thus been invaluable to archaeologists trying to reconstruct life at that time. It presents a picture of a complicated society that relied on legal experts to keep things running smoothly. Historians know this because the code itself described the certification of professionals such as doctors, craftsmen, judges, and lawyers.

Old Testament

Around this same time the events of the early part of the Old Testament were happening to the west of Babylon. The Ten Commandments were one of the earliest sets of laws used by the Israelites. They were said to be given to the prophet Moses by God. These laws provided a basic set of guidelines by which people should live. Some of the commandments are still central to today's legal system, such as prohibitions against killing and theft.

Later in the history of Israel, people called judges became the leaders of the Israelites. The judges created laws and resolved disputes among the people. Most of them were men, but there was at least one famous female judge, named Deborah. Deborah is said to have worked sitting under a palm tree, where she listened to disputes and rendered her judgments in verse.

Ancient Greece

Some historians credit the lawmaker Solon with laying the foundations for the democratic government of Athens. Solon was the leader of Athens during the mid-500s B.C.E. He reportedly took control of the city during a time of conflict between the nobility and the common folk and among the peoples of various regions. His solution to these problems was to write laws. In these laws, he created an assembly of citizens to make decisions for the city, and the Heliaea, or people's court. He also divided the citizenry into four classes for

Problem
Solving

The jurors were in charge of keeping time during trials to ensure that both plaintiffs and defendants had equal time to speak. But how could they tell how much time had passed without a clock? With a water clock! One juror, chosen by lot, would pour a specific amount of water into a large jar when a speaker began to speak. The water would run out of this jar in a steady stream. When the jar was empty, the speaker's time was up. The amount of water poured into the clock varied according to the significance of the matter at hand—the more important the case, the longer the speakers were given.

After both sides in a case had given their speeches, jurors voted. Each juror had two ballots, one representing the plaintiff and the other representing the defendant. They lined up and placed their vote in a bronze urn, discarding the other ballot in a wooden one. After each juror voted, he was given a token that he could use to redeem his juror's fee. After the voting, the courtroom attendants would empty the bronze urn in full view of both parties to the lawsuit and count the ballots. Whichever side received the most votes won.

purposes of taxation, created rules to help people find work, sell their goods, and improve foreign trade, and ended the enslavement of debtors.

Ancient Athenians brought their complaints to the Helieaea, the people's court, and to other courts where juries of citizens would listen to cases, vote on the outcome, and vote on punishments for those found guilty. There were no judges, only juries. Athenian courts heard both civil and criminal matters, as well as appeals from citizens who were dissatisfied with rulings by the council or the assembly. Athenian juries were set up to further the democratic ideals of the city; any citizen who did not owe a debt to the treasury, who was at least thirty years old, and who had never lost his citizenship could serve as a juror. To further encourage participation, Athens paid its jurors, which made it possible for poorer men to serve. Athens went to great lengths to ensure that its juries were not bribed.

Ancient Rome

Ancient Romans were obsessed with law. Romans of all social classes participated in their government and followed the events of the courts. Every Roman man of the upper classes was at least in part a lawyer, and there is some evidence that women of the same class were also fairly well-versed in the law. Wealthy Roman men acted as "patrons," which meant that they helped out a group of less-well-off families called "clients" and in return could expect support from those families. As patrons, they wrote wills, lent money, arbitrated disputes, and handled any other legal problems their clients presented. If a client got sued, the patron would represent him in court. Trials were a form of public entertainment, and Roman noblemen spent years studying rhetoric so that they could deliver spellbinding speeches. Roman noblemen were also expected to hold various elected public offices and serve as legislators.

The Roman Republic began in 510 B.C.E. with the overthrow of the monarchy. The republic took its name from its republican form of government. The word "republic" comes from the Latin words "res publica," which means "public thing." It was based on the concept of public law and served as the foundation for the Roman constitution. The constitution encoded such principles as elections, separation of powers, checks and balances, vetoes, and term limits. This constitution was never written down as one document, but its principles were well known and widely accepted, and eventually found their way into the U.S. Constitution.

Fast Facts

When a Roman wrote a will, he brought it to the Temple of the Vestal Virgins. The Vestals were women who had promised to remain virgins while serving as priestesses of Vesta, goddess of the hearth. Their chief duty was to tend the sacred flame, but they also cared for the wills of all Roman citizens.

One of the earliest sets of Roman laws was the twelve tables, which date to the mid-400s B.C.E. According to Roman historians, an official of the time decided that the law should be written so that it could be applied fairly to all cases. A delegation traveled to Athens to copy the law of Solon. Those laws ended up on twelve stone tablets, hence the "twelve tables."

Around 31 B.C.E. a civil war dissolved the republic and began the empire, during which the emperor became the supreme ruler. The senate continued to meet, and an advisory body of senators and nobles called the *consilium principis* assisted the emperor, but ultimately he had total power. He could create laws and served as the judge of the ultimate court.

As a practical matter, however, local people tended to govern themselves using Roman legal principles. The empire was huge, with provinces all over Europe, Africa, and Asia. Leadership from Rome was inconsistent and unstable; emperors were regularly deposed, and occasionally the army took over. Most provinces were really governed by local bodies. Officials from Roman visiting provinces primarily concerned themselves with censuses and tax collection. Local officials handled criminal justice, public works, religious festivals, and diplomatic relations with Romans.

The Roman empire effectively ended around 476 C.E., but its legal influence continued for centuries more in the East. Between 529 and 534 the Byzantine emperor Justinian compiled the *Corpus Juris Civilis* (Body of Civil Law), a collection of all known imperial Roman laws dating back to the emperor Hadrian (76-138). The corpus included several constitutions of the Roman emperors. It united the state and the Orthodox Church, outlawed heresy and pagan practices, and stated that only Christians could be citizens.

Medieval Europe

Though Rome's reach was wide, the peoples who lived north of the Roman empire created their own sets of laws that eventually evolved into the common law. Germans and Celts developed legal practices that emphasized the role of judges and tradition more than written legal codes. The laws of the Catholic Church and the now-defunct Roman empire were combined with Germanic traditions to create the English common law.

Celtic Laws

In northern Europe, the Celtic people created their own set of laws. Historians believe that the Celts developed these laws between 2300 and 900 B.C.E., but they don't know exactly when because the laws were not written. Instead, legal experts memorized them and served as legal advisers and arbitrators. These laws formed the basis of Ireland's Brehon laws, which were finally written down in the 600s C.E. Celtic law divided people into five social classes, from kings and nobles to slaves. These people were then organized into groups. Everyone was a member of a family, which was a member of a clan, which was a member of a tribe, which belonged to a kingdom. Every tribe owed allegiance to its ruler, paid in property and military help.

Legal experts were especially crucial for handling responses to crimes. Celtic laws did away with the ancient practice of retaliation for crimes and replaced it with a scheme of compensation designed to end disputes peacefully. If a person harmed another, the victim or the victim's family would bring the case before a chief and a legal expert. The legal expert would listen to the facts and decide the appropriate punishment. Every crime merited a specific compensation; cutting off a person's hand earned a smaller fine than murder would. Petty disputes went to the courts of local chiefs, while major disputes might go all the way to a king. A party who brought a case to court had to bring at least two witnesses to testify on his behalf. Social rank was important in courts; a person of lower rank could not always testify against someone of higher class. Celtic law almost never used capital punishment.

German Laws

Germanic peoples did not compile legal codes until the end of the Roman Empire, instead using custom to determine how to settle disputes and deal with criminals. Germanic tribes periodically assembled at a festival called the "Thing," at which they settled disputes, traded goods, and arranged marriages. Anyone who believed he had suffered a grievance would wait until the Thing, and then present his case before the king, who acted as judge. Both parties could speak and present witnesses, and the king would issue a judgment. Community pressure dictated that parties abide by the judgment and refrain from solving their own problems by force.

German laws covered many different types of crime. Stealing cattle was a serious offense, and penalties varied depending on the value of the cattle stolen; a bull owned by the king merited a higher fine than a bull that serviced only the cows of a single herd owned by an ordinary man. Stealing an object that lay outside a house was not as serious as breaking into a house to steal. Rape, assault, insult, and murder were all criminal offenses punishable by fines. Tribes set fines according to the value of the victim. Killing a pregnant woman merited a higher fine than killing a woman past her childbearing years. If a murderer concealed his victim in an attempt to hide his crime the punishment was greater than if he did not. A murderer who did not have enough money to pay the fine was expected to ask his relatives and friends for help. If he still could not raise enough money, he might be executed.

Germanic inheritance law favored male heirs. If a father died and left sons, they would inherit his property. If he had no sons, then his property would go to his parents, his siblings, or his relatives on his father's side. In most cases, the inheritance could not go to a woman.

English Law: Common Law

The English common law, which forms the main basis for the American legal system, developed out of Germanic legal traditions. Germanic law arrived in the British Isles when a Germanic people called the Anglo-Saxons sailed to England from Germany and Denmark during the 400s and quickly dominated the Celtic locals. In creating their legal system, the Anglo-Saxons were influenced by Roman law, Christian principles, and their own Germanic traditions.

Anglo-Saxons emphasized loyalty to one's own lord, to the king, to the church, and especially to one's family. They took oaths extremely seriously. Violence was apparently a major problem, if literature of the period is to be believed, and the Anglo-Saxon legal system was designed to maintain order. All freemen took an oath at the age of 12, swearing to abstain from and denounce all major crimes. Anyone who committed a crime had not only done wrong, but he had also broken his oath, which was considered an act of disloyalty to the community. A criminal did not just bring opprobrium upon himself, but upon his whole family, and the entire family could be punished for a crime committed by one of its members.

Around 600, the Anglo-Saxons broke with their tradition of transmitting all laws orally and began putting laws into writing when King Ethelbert of Kent issued the first known written legal code. This code listed crimes and their accompanying fines. The worst punishments were reserved for crimes against church property or priests.

Ethelbert's code was followed by a number of other written legal codes produced over the next four centuries by kings and their councils. These codes most likely were not "new" laws but simply written versions of rules that Germanic peoples had used for centuries.

Anglo-Saxon Courts

The Anglo-Saxons set up a series of courts throughout the land, with major courts in each shire and borough and smaller local courts known as "hundred" courts. The king appointed officials to preside over these courts. The officials of hundred courts, assisted by the families of victims, would track down accused criminals and bring them back to the courts to hear the cases against them.

A plaintiff bringing a lawsuit before an Anglo-Saxon court had to follow strict rules of procedure. Any procedural error could cause the lawsuit to be dismissed, which is still the case in the United States today. The plaintiff began the lawsuit by appearing before the hundred court, swearing an oath, making a statement before witnesses, and summoning the defendant to come to court to answer the charges. The judge of the court would then decide if the plaintiff's case was sufficient to merit a trial, and whether his court had jurisdiction. He might dismiss the case then or transfer it to the higher shire court. If the judge accepted the case, he would set a date on which the defendant was to appear.

On the court date, if the defendant appeared, the plaintiff would repeat his charge and the defendant would answer it. A defendant would often respond simply by swearing that he had not committed the crime in question, and would call upon friends to swear that his oath was true. This was often enough for a defendant to go free. Some historians believe this system worked mainly because the population attending a hundred court was small, the individuals all knew one another and had to live together, and were not likely to lie. A defendant who was known to be guilty would be unable to find supporters to swear that his oath was true, and would likely be found guilty.

If a judge decided an accused was guilty, he would set a punishment, which might extend to the convict's kinsmen. Punishments included fines, physical mutilation, execution, or exile, sometimes of an entire family. Capital punishment was not uncommon, and apparently became a cause for concern. Around 930, King Aethelstan raised the age of criminal responsibility from 12 to 16 because he thought it was cruel to execute young people for crimes such as stealing sheep.

Later English Courts

In 1066, the Normans from France, led by William the Conqueror, conquered England. This change in government led to a gradual change in the legal system and the emergence of what is known as "common law." King Henry II (1154-1189) created a national legal system that was common to the entire country. He appointed judges to a central court and then sent them throughout the country to hear cases. A judge would resolve a case based on his interpretation of local custom and practices. He would then return to London and file his decision. These royal judges often discussed cases with one another and started to use previous decisions as the basis for deciding their cases. Older decisions, or precedents, took on the force of law. This is a legal principle known as *stare decisis*. Eventually, a judge was bound to use another judge's earlier interpretation of the law if the facts before him were the same or very similar. The result was that after a few centuries, all of England really did have a body of laws that was "common" to all regions.

Over the centuries, England developed another court system that functioned as a sort of parallel system to the common law courts. These courts were called "equity courts," and common law courts were called "courts of law." By tradition, courts of law could award only monetary damages, and could only recognize the official, legal owner of property. The difficulty with this system was that decisions were sometimes too harsh. Equity courts did not use juries, only judges. Courts of equity could apply "natural law" to produce results that were more practical and often seen to be more fair. Courts of equity applied principles of fairness and flexibility as opposed to precedent and statutory law. Courts of equity could issue injunctions; for example, they could order a party to do something or stop doing something. They could also recognize trusts. Equity courts therefore became involved in many property issues, deciding cases in which more than one person had a right to a given piece of property. This bifurcated system traveled to the United States, where many states to this day maintain courts of equity alongside courts of law. (The Seventh Amendment of the U.S. Constitution guarantees a jury trial in "suits at common law," but not in suits at equity.)

The Parliament of England came into existence in the early 1200s, but it was centuries before it assumed the legislative role it holds today. Initially the parliament was a group of nobles summoned by the king to help him raise taxes. Gradually the group took on a more advisory role. During the 16th century, Parliament took on the job of writing bills and presenting them to the monarch for signature or veto. Bills that were signed became laws. These laws formed the basis of statutory law, which functioned together with common law as the body of English law.

In England, practitioners of law divided themselves into two basic groups, barristers and solicitors. Barristers specialized in arguing cases in front of judges and juries. Solicitors handled research, often doing the research and writing briefs for barristers, and wrote documents such as contracts.

Continental Law: Civil Law

Civil law, also known as continental law, developed out of Roman law. Medieval lawyers had continued to use the *Corpus Juris Civilis* and other later codes of laws, but they also used precedents and custom to create law as needed. No European nation had a uniform set of laws. In the 17th and 18th centuries, scholars in France and Germany began to explore the concepts of democracy and the rule of law. They decided that the only way to ensure that law was applied consistently was to compile all laws into codes.

The French emperor Napoleon created the French civil code, called the Napoleonic Code, in 1804. This was part of Napoleon's effort to reform the French state and create a modern nation. The Napoleonic Code insisted that law must come from the legislature, and limited judges' power to make case law. Under the code, laws could be applied only if they had been passed by the legislature and officially published. The code set rules for citizenship, property ownership, and family matters; in particular, it made divorce fairly easy for both men and women to obtain.

In civil law countries, specialized workers emerged to do various legal tasks. Some men worked as advocates who were licensed to argue cases in court. Others did legal research and interpreted laws, wrote documents such as wills and contracts, or served as notaries, clerks, or scriveners, witnessing documents and filling out forms for clients.

Law in the United States

The people who colonized the United States brought their legal systems with them. The inhabitants of the original thirteen colonies adopted the law of England. French and Spanish settlers claimed much of the southeastern, central, and southwestern United States. Those early settlers left their mark on certain state legal systems. Louisiana is the most notable of these examples, but there are traces of civil law in other states as well.

Common Law

The settlers of the thirteen colonies used the example of their mother country for devising their own systems of laws. All of them took from England the practice of common law. American judges became major creators of American law through hearing cases and making decisions. They followed the English principle of *stare decisis*, using previous court decisions as rules to guide subsequent ones. They also adopted some pre-Revolutionary British statutes, particularly statutes dealing with fraudulent transactions.

The Constitution: Foundation of U.S. Law

As everyone knows from their elementary school days, by the late 1700s the American colonists were tired of British rule and rebelled against it. Law and lawyers were at the heart of this rebellion. The Declaration of Independence, the 1776 document announcing that the thirteen colonies were independent states no longer part of the British Empire, was written mainly by Thomas Jefferson, a lawyer from Virginia. Jefferson spent years practicing law and serving as a representative in the Virginia House of Burgesses. A student of Enlightenment thought, Jefferson embraced the idea of natural law, which he believed gave the colonists the right to govern themselves. At the Second Continental Congress in 1775, Jefferson was given the job of writing a document that would explain why the colonists believed they should be independent. He wrote the Declaration of Independence, the document that specifies exactly how Americans thought of themselves: equal and endowed with the rights to life, liberty, and the pursuit of happiness.

In 1787, the now-free Americans decided they needed to decide exactly how the government of their new country would work. They created the U.S. Constitution, which defines the shape of the federal government of the United States and more than any other document forms the basis of American law. The Constitution established the three branches of the government—legislative, executive, and judicial—and specified the rights of each of these, reserving all other rights for the states. Since its ratification, the Constitution has been amended 27 times, to address such topics as searches and seizures and the right to bear arms, to extend the right to vote to blacks and women, and to establish the income tax. The U.S. Supreme Court holds the power of judicial review, evaluating laws passed by legislatures to see that they meet the requirements of the Constitution. As states joined the union, they created their own constitutions, many of them patterned on the U.S. Constitution.

Civil Law in the United States

France sold the Louisiana territory to the United States in 1803 in the transaction known as the Louisiana Purchase. The people of Louisiana, however, were still predominantly French, and they organized their legal system according to French principles. They divided the state into parishes instead of counties. The state still has a civil code that governs most aspects of life, including marriage, inheritance, property, contracts, and civil procedure. The state gradually incorporated some aspects of common law, such as the use of precedent, but the authority of judges to create law has never been as strong in Louisiana as it is in the rest of the United States.

Several other states have kept certain aspects of civil law despite the fact that they are primarily common law jurisdictions. Civil law mainly appears in these states' treatment of marital property.

Lawyers in the United States

Law has traditionally been a fairly respectable profession that attracted the sons of wealthy families. Lawyers in the 1700s and 1800s tended to come from families with enough money to educate them. Before a boy could study law, he had to be able to read well, in Latin as well as in English, which meant he had to have spent his childhood either going to school or working with a tutor. Early colleges and universities did not teach law; a young man would take a degree in some other subject, such as philosophy, and then "read law" with a practitioner. He would spend this apprenticeship studying cases, performing research, drafting documents, and performing other tasks that prepared him to practice law on his own. There was no specific curriculum, though most would-be lawyers read certain treatises on English law such as William Blackstone's *Commentaries on the Laws of England*. Abraham Lincoln reportedly read the necessary books on his own without apprenticing himself to another lawyer. Eventually a new lawyer would be admitted to the state bar and allowed to take on his own clients.

Fast Facts

Many residents of Louisiana believe that the Napoleonic Code is the law of the state, but they are wrong. The Napoleonic Code was never the official law in Louisiana, because it was enacted in 1804, after France had sold the territory. That means that in the play *A Streetcar Named Desire*, Stanley Kowalski is mistaken when he says that the Napoleonic Code applies to his marriage. He was right about the community property aspects, though.

Most early lawyers were jacks-of-all-trades. They would argue cases in court, both civil and criminal, and they might represent both plaintiffs and defendants. They would also draft wills, write contracts, handle domestic disputes such as divorces, and take on any other tasks for which they could charge clients. Many lawyers doubled as politicians, serving in legislatures.

Organization of the Profession

In the late 1800s law began transforming into the profession it is today. The American Bar Association formed in 1878 to create uniform standards and ethical rules for lawyers. In the 1890s, the ABA urged state bars to set rules for admission that required attorneys to have earned an academic degree in law. Around this time colleges and universities were rapidly proliferating throughout the country and many of them were opening law schools. The requirements for entering the profession gradually became stiffer. Law school expanded from two to three years and raised admission standards.

Part of the ABA's mission was to regulate the legal profession. They did this by making it more difficult to become a lawyer, which kept down the numbers of aspirants to the field. This made it easier for existing lawyers to make a living and ensured that the quality of those lawyers who did enter the profession was relatively consistent. In the two decades after World War II, the number of law school graduates remained stable, producing a steady but hardly overwhelming supply of new lawyers. By the 1960s, however, more and more people were demanding an opportunity to become attorneys. Men who had gone to college through the G.I. bill, the educated children of baby boomers, and especially women and racial minorities aspired to become lawyers. Law schools increased their enrollments in the 1960s and 1970s, and new law schools opened, which quickly increased the number of attorneys in the United States.

Some of these attorneys were absorbed into criminal practice, where new laws guaranteeing legal defense to all criminal defendants resulted in the creation of new public defender offices. Attorneys in private practice had to work to find new clients who could employ them. They managed to find business, but rounding up new clients, or rainmaking, has since then been one of the big challenges of legal practice. It was around this time that the billable hour became the standard method of legal billing in private practice. In 1958 the ABA had published a pamphlet encouraging attorneys to keep track of the hours they worked, claiming that attorneys' flagging earnings were directly related to their incompetent business practices. By the 1970s this had turned into hourly billing.

The Rise of the Billable Hour

The billable hour is a fairly recent development in the law. Until the 1960s, lawyers earned their money through specific fees for specific services such as writing wills, retainers, bonuses from satisfied clients, and fees paid by the losers in court cases. State laws set limits on legal fees. The ABA's Model Rules of Professional Responsibility listed several guidelines for setting fees, recommending that lawyers consider the difficulty of the work, the likelihood that the lawyer would have to forego other work, time limitations, experience of the lawyer, and several other factors including time and labor involved.

During the 1960s, lawyers gradually began keeping track of the time they spent during the day. Law firm consultants around that time suggested that lawyers who kept accurate time records and billed by the hour made more money than attorneys who set fees through other methods. By the late 1960s most large and mid-sized firms had moved to hourly billing. Firms began to base their budgets on the number of hours they expected to bill at certain rates.

Law firms initially set fairly reasonable expectations for hours billed. In the 1970s and 1980s, lawyers were expected to bill between 1500 and 1700 hours per year. (If you work 40 hours per week for 50 weeks of a year, taking about two weeks off, you will have worked 2000 hours in that year.) But the implications of hourly billing are obvious: in order to make more money, a firm must either increase its hourly rates or it must bill more hours. Increasing hourly rates does happen, but clients protest if rates get too high, so much of the burden for increasing income falls on the shoulders of attorneys and paralegals who must work more hours.

During the 1990s, billable requirements climbed higher and higher. Today it is not uncommon for law firms to require associates to bill between 1800 and 2300 hours per year. A number such as 1800 hours might even be considered a "part-time" schedule. Because not every hour worked is a billable hour—firm meetings, some travel, pro bono work, time spent talking with colleagues—lawyers must work many more hours than their billable requirements in order to hit their goals. Attorneys and paralegals find themselves recording every act they do during the workday in 15 or even six-minute increments. Some firms award bonuses to attorneys who exceed their billable hour requirements. Others penalize those who fall short.

Women in the Law

Women have only recently been admitted to the legal profession. Early in the 20th century a few pioneering women tried to become lawyers, but it was very difficult because most law schools admitted only men. It wasn't until the 1960s and 1970s that law schools opened their doors to female students. (Even then equality was still out of reach; Harvard Law School professors in the 1960s would hold "Ladies Days," in which they would call exclusively on female students to answer questions about cases involving underwear and other embarrassing topics.) These numbers have changed rapidly over the past four decades, and now women make up about half of all law students and a huge proportion of legal staff workers.

Skyrocketing Salaries

Between 2000 and 2007, salaries at top law firms increased dramatically. Law firms entered a kind of arms race, all competing for the best law school graduates. If one major firm raised its salary

---

INTERVIEW

Perspectives on Changes in the Law

Frank Wagar
Attorney, Covington, Louisiana

How many years did you practice law?
30.

What did you do in your practice?
Labor and employment law.

Whom did you work for?
I worked for a number of private firms and then became in-house counsel for the power company Entergy. I liked in-house corporate practice better than law firm practice. Hours were one factor. Also, to my mind I had a little more professional freedom.

Can you say a little bit about what law school was like?
I think the big difference between law school then and now is that when I was there we saw no clinics as there are at virtually all law schools. Law school was all theoretical. Clinics today give law students a chance to get some practical experience before graduation. I think this is a good change. I believe until the late 1950s in Louisiana you didn't have to go to law school, you could apprentice for a while. Some fellows came into law school without having completed their under-graduate degrees; that was allowed at the time.

When you graduated from law school, what sort of jobs did you and your classmates get? What was a typical starting salary?
It really depended on your class standing. The lower in the class, the more difficult it was to get a job with a firm, but most people did go into the practice of law. I don't know of anyone who went into solo practice right out of school, but there were a number of fellows who went into practice with one or two other attorneys and split the in-come on a percentage basis. If you were on law review or moot court, you had opportunities to work for judges. Starting salaries—I started at around $15,000, I think, or less. I know it wasn't above $15,000. It was probably more like $10,000, to be honest. And I was on law review, and you generally tended to get higher salary offers if you were on law review. I would say the average was probably somewhere around $7,500 or $8,000.

How did you do legal research?

It was all books. If there were computers, they were hidden away in Washington somewhere, in the Department of Defense.

What about writing documents—did you use yellow pads, dictaphones, and that sort of thing?

Yes, we used yellow pads, dictaphones, and all that. In private practice, I started out writing documents by hand, but some of the senior partners thought that was not efficient and encouraged me, so I started to use dictaphones. It was hard to get used to, but eventually it did prove to be a time saver.

Did law firms place the same emphasis on billing a certain number of hours that they do now? Did you notice the rise of the billable hour as it was happening?

I don't know it was the same emphasis, but yeah, there was emphasis on billable hours. You were supposed to bill around 1,700 to 2,000 hours. After about five years of law firm practice I said, you know, I really don't like this nonsense and I got out and moved to an in-house position. I've heard it's gotten worse from people who practice.

What about women? Were there any in your law school class? When did you start to see female lawyers in real numbers?

I know there was one, and I think she was the only one but there might have been two. We excused her presence because her father was an attorney, or at least this explained her deviant behavior. If she had any problems, I was not aware of them. Some guys would ask what she was doing here, but I don't think they harassed her—they were just puzzled by this strange creature.

What about paralegals? Did you work with them when you first started? Did they ever play much of a role at Entergy?

There were no paralegals when I started practicing. At Entergy for the last ten years I worked there they played a big role. Most of the paralegals I dealt with were very, very good. Unless you're really committed to the actual practice of law, being a paralegal is a good career in and of itself.

What sort of changes have you seen in what is expected of attorneys, and what attorneys expect out of their profession?

I don't know if the people who went into law changed after the sixties or early seventies, but there was a loss, for me, anyway, of professional courtesy and collegiality. It was sort of like, "what answer does the client want," and that's the answer attorneys gave, particularly in the securities and corporate areas.

for summer associates or first-year associates, all the other major firms would do the same. This resulted in salary increases of thousands of dollars every year. At the same time, the pressure to bill an astronomical number of hours became ever more intense. Every year certain observers and participants would call for an end to the madness, pointing out that there are only so many hours in a year and that unbridled billing pressure could lead only to total enslavement to the job and probably to unethical behavior. None of these voices crying in the wilderness had much effect on the escalation of salaries and billing requirements. Some experts expressed hope that the recession of 2008-09 would ease the pressure to bill more hours. They predicted that clients would finally refuse to pay hourly rates, forcing law firms to come up with new billing methods, which could then allow lawyers to focus on working efficiently instead of working longer.

Paralegals Appear

Though lawyers have always used secretaries and clerks to help them prepare documents, paralegals did not appear until the 1970s. Around this time, lawyers started to use staff people to do real legal research and other work that required a greater knowledge of the law than that needed by secretaries. The National Federation of Paralegal Associations, founded in 1974, was the first national paralegal association. This organization and others have spent the past three decades trying to formalize the role of paralegals and create standards for non-lawyers in legal practice. Today there is still no formal definition of a paralegal, and there are few genuine certifications. Basically anyone who can persuade an attorney to hire him or her can be a paralegal. Paralegals and legal assistants may be poised to take a much bigger role in legal practice; the Bureau of Labor Statistics predicts that growth in the paralegal field will be very rapid in the near future as purchasers of legal services look for ways to avoid paying lawyers exorbitant fees for their work.

What Happens Next?

The 1990s and 2000s were a period of rapid change in the law. During that time, lawyers moved from an entirely paper-based practice (in the late 1990s, many lawyers were still using dictaphones and yellow pads to compose documents) to one that is heavily computer based. Technology has created new legal specialties such as litigation technology and e-discovery. Competition from overseas legal firms and other sources is putting pressure on legal professionals at all levels. It remains to be seen whether law will continue to be a hot field attracting top graduates.

What is certain, however, is that there will always be a demand for attorneys and legal experts. Laws will always be with us, and so will lawyers.

A Brief Chronology

1760 B.C.E.: Hammurabi unites several kingdoms into the Babylonian Empire in present-day Iraq and establishes code of common laws.

c.1400 B.C.E.: Moses receives the Ten Commandments on Mount Sinai.

590 B.C.E.: Solon implements democratic principles and institutions into the civic life of Athens, including the Helieaea, or people's court.

c.450 B.C.E.: The twelve tables, one of the earliest sets of Roman laws, are created.

400–500 C.E.: Anglo-Saxons sail to England and overtake Celtic locals, creating an oral legal system influenced by Roman law, Christian teachings, and Germanic traditions.

c.500: After the fall of the Roman Empire in 476, Germanic peoples begin compiling legal codes.

534: Byzantine emperor Justinian completes his Corpus *Juris Civilis* (Body of Civil Law).

600: Anglo-Saxons begin putting laws into writing when King Ethelbert of Kent issues first known written legal code.

600–700: Ireland's Brehon laws, a compilation of ancient Celtic laws dating back to 2300 B.C.E., are officially recorded.

1066: William the Conqueror leads Normans from France to conquer England, resulting in the emergence of "common law."

1180: King Henry II of England creates national legal system common to entire country.

1200: Parliament of England comes into being.

1600–1700: Scholars in France and Germany come to a consensus that laws must be compiled into codes to function effectively.

1700: Parliament of England expands its role to take on the job of writing bills and presenting them to the monarch for signature or veto.

1775: Thomas Jefferson writes Declaration of Independence for the Second Continental Congress of American colonists, explaining why British colonial subjects should be independent.

1776: Declaration of Independence ratified, granting sovereignty of the thirteen colonies from the British Empire.

1787: United States Constitution written and adopted.

1804: The French emperor Napoleon creates the French civil code, called the Napoleonic Code.

1878: American Bar Association formed.

1890: American Bar Association requires attorneys earn an academic degree in law.

1944: G.I. Bill passed, making it possible for thousands of ex-servicemen to addend college and, eventually, law school.

1958: American Bar Association publishes pamphlet encouraging lawyers to keep track of hours worked.

1960–1970: New law schools opened to meet increased demands of those wishing to become attorneys, particularly among racial minorities and women.

1970: Lawyers adopt practice of hourly billing.

1974: The National Federation of Paralegal Associations, the first national paralegal association, is founded.

1990–present: Increased use of technology leads to new areas of specialization for lawyers, such as intellectual property and e-discovery. As smaller firms begin to merge, a consistent rise of corporate law firms.

Chapter 2

State of the Industry

A lawyer, or attorney, is a person who is licensed to practice law. What exactly does that mean? It can mean many things, but in general lawyers do the following tasks:

➡ Provide legal advice to clients;

➡ Represent clients (both in person and in writing) in court and in administrative hearings, through oral arguments, pleadings, and briefs;

➡ Research legal questions and support arguments with that research;

➡ Negotiate and draft contracts;

➡ Draft wills, create trusts, and administer the estates of the deceased;

➡ Protect intellectual property; and

➡ Accept clients and set fees.

Lawyers may handle civil or criminal cases. An attorney may spend all her time in an office reviewing documents or hit the road on a daily basis to visit clients, attend hearings, and appear in court. Some lawyers work insane hours; others manage to create profitable part-time practices.

Attorneys do not work alone. Supporting them are armies of personnel, including paralegals and legal assistants, legal secretaries, litigation technology specialists, law librarians, and office managers.

The legal field grew rapidly at the end of the 20th century, drawing thousands of workers attracted by the prospect of good money and prestige. After years of skyrocketing salaries, though, growth in the legal profession has been slowing down. Competition from paralegals and the reluctance of clients to pay massive legal fees based on the billable hour may be changing the way the legal profession works. The introduction of technology into discovery and research has created new legal specialties and forced attorneys to reconsider the way they charge for their services.

Though the legal profession is still fairly strong, as of 2009 growth had become slow for attorneys. Paralegals are in higher demand but competition is fierce.

The Judicial System

In the United States, there are two main kinds of court, federal and state. They differ in the types of lawsuits that can be brought before them. If a matter is based on state law, it will go to a state court. If it is based on federal law, it goes to federal court. At both the federal and state levels, there are two main types of court, trial courts and courts of appeals.

Which court an attorney chooses depends on a principle called "jurisdiction." Jurisdiction is a court's or judge's power to investigate the facts of a matter, apply law to them, and declare a judgment. It also refers to the geographic territory in which a court can exercise its authority. The vast majority of lawsuits, including all criminal lawsuits, start in state court. Federal courts are established by the Constitution, which specifies the cases that they may hear. Federal matters include discrimination (issues such as sexual harassment or race discrimination), cases in which the parties come from different states, bankruptcy, and questions of international law.

When choosing a court, an attorney must consider three criteria. First, does the court have jurisdiction over a matter? In other words, can it hear this type of case? Second, is the court in the right place? Does the defendant live within its geographic territory, or did the incident happen in that territory? Third, does the court have personal jurisdiction over the defendant? In other words, can it enforce a judgment against the defendant? Filing a lawsuit with the wrong court is a major mistake; it happens, but it looks very bad and attorneys do their best to avoid it.

First-year law students spend months agonizing over the intricacies of jurisdiction. What you should know is that there are two main types: subject matter jurisdiction and personal jurisdiction. "Subject-matter jurisdiction" refers to a court's power to hear a particular type of case. The many different federal, state, and local courts all hear different types of cases. Federal courts hear cases involving federal laws. State and local courts hear both civil and criminal cases, sometimes dividing who hears what based on the amount of money in controversy. Bankruptcy courts hear bankruptcy cases.

"Personal jurisdiction" refers to a court's power over a particular defendant or piece of property. Not every court can go after every defendant. There has to be some geographic connection between court and defendant, partly so that local law enforcement will have power over the defendant if needed. For example, a state court can typically only try cases involving defendants who live in or do business within the state.

Trial Court

The trial court level is where most lawsuits are filed. Trial courts are called different names in different states: county court, district court, court of common pleas, or circuit court. (In New York, a trial court is called a "supreme court" for extra confusion.) Trial courts also include traffic court, family court, juvenile court, probate court, and many others. At the federal level, trial courts are called "district courts."

At trial, the party bringing the lawsuit is called the "plaintiff." The party defending itself is called the "defendant." In civil cases, both plaintiff and defendant are private citizens. In criminal cases, the government brings a lawsuit against a person accused of a crime, who is also called a defendant. When you read the name of a court case, the first party listed is the plaintiff; the one after the "v." is the defendant. In other words, a case name will be written *"Plaintiff v. Defendant."*

The trial court determines questions of fact and questions of law. Questions of fact concern what exactly happened in the case before the court. Who did what to whom? When did all of it happen? The lawyers presenting the case use various types of evidence to establish the facts that they want the judge or jury to believe. They will ask questions of the parties and witnesses, show exhibits, and make speeches in which they try to convince the judge or jury that their side is correct. Questions of law concern which law applies to the case. This includes both substantive law, i.e. the law that governs the facts of the matter, and procedural law, i.e. how the case should be tried, which court should hear it, the proper parties, etc.

At trial, the "factfinder" decides which facts are relevant and determines whether the plaintiff has met the burden of proof. The factfinder can be either a judge or a jury. If a judge makes the decision, the trial is called a "bench trial." If a jury decides, it is called a "jury trial." The judge presiding over the trial then makes a final decision, called a judgment. The judgment is the amount of money or other remedy awarded to the prevailing party by the court.

Appellate Court (Court of Appeals)

If a party to a lawsuit is unhappy with the trial court's decision, he or she can appeal to a higher court. These higher courts are known as appellate courts, or courts of appeals. An appeals court considers only questions of law, i.e. whether the trial court applied the law correctly to the facts. The appeals court uses the facts that were established at trial, as set forth in the record of the trial. That means that an appeal does not involve exhibits of evidence or cross-examination of witnesses. Instead, the lawyers for the parties present written briefs and oral arguments in which they try to convince the judges that the trial court applied the law improperly, made a procedural error, reached a verdict not supported by the weight of the evidence, or committed another legal error.

The party who brings the appeal is called the "appellant" and the other party the "respondent." The appellant's name is listed first in the case citation, i.e. *"Appellant v. Respondent."* Judges at the appeals level are sometimes called "justices."

In the federal court system, there are two levels of appeals court. Circuit courts of appeal handle appeals from federal district courts. There are 13 judicial circuits within the United States, each of them covering several states. Above the circuit courts is the U.S. Supreme Court. If a party believes that a circuit court has decided its case wrongly, that party can try to appeal to the Supreme Court. The nine justices of the Supreme Court hear very few cases every year. They select only cases that they believe will have a significant impact on the nation's interpretation of constitutional law.

At the state level, there are many different appeals structures. Some states have an intermediate appeals court, for first appeals. If a party does not like the decision of the first appeals court, it can appeal to the state's highest court. The highest court is called "supreme court" in most states, but not all of them.

The decisions that come out of appeals are very important. After a judge hears a case, he or she writes an explanation of his or her decision. This document examines the statutory law and case law that applies to the matter, considers the decisions past courts have made in similar situations, and explains the judge's reasoning in arriving at a decision. From then on, lawyers and other judges will read this decision and use it in formulating their legal arguments. The decision will become a "precedent" and will effectively function as established law.

Stages of a Civil Lawsuit

The litigation of a lawsuit is a long, complicated, expensive process involving a number of different stages. Some lawsuits take years to reach their conclusion.

Pleading

A lawsuit begins with pleadings, the documents in which each party states its position on the matter.

Complaint

The complaint is the document that starts the ball rolling. A person with a grievance goes to see a lawyer to decide whether it is worth suing someone else. The attorney will ask about the facts, check the statute of limitations to make sure the injury did not happen too long ago, research the law, and decide whether any damages could be forthcoming. The attorney must also decide where to file the lawsuit, i.e. in city, state, or federal court. If the case looks promising, the attorney will draft a complaint, which describes the facts of the matter and lists the causes of action (i.e., legal grounds for suing) upon which the client, now called a plaintiff, hopes to recover. The attorney files the complaint with the court and delivers (serves) it to the person being sued, who now discovers that he or she is a defendant to a lawsuit.

Answer

The defendant is given a fairly short time in which to respond to the allegations in the complaint. This is done in a document called an answer, in which the defendant confirms or denies the allegations and proposes any affirmative defenses to the claims. Most defendants hire lawyers to do this work, though that is not necessary.

Discovery

One reason that lawsuits take as long as they do is that it takes a long time to investigate the facts and gather evidence to support or defend a case. This process is called discovery, or pre-trial discovery.

Interrogatories

Interrogatories are written questions sent from plaintiff to defendant and vice versa (or, more usually, attorney to attorney). Each side is supposed to answer these questions within a certain time limit.

Document Review

Document review is the process of reading documents (letters, e-mails, sales records, or building plans, for example) created and owned by the opposing side, hoping to find something incriminating. This process can take an extraordinarily long time. Sometimes defendants produce massive piles of documents that lawyers and their assistants must sift through. Usually they try to avoid producing anything that looks bad, claiming privilege when possible.

Depositions

Depositions are face-to-face (or telephone) interviews with witnesses or parties to the lawsuit, conducted under oath and recorded by a court reporter. Depositions give attorneys a chance to meet the plaintiff or witnesses and question them about their knowledge of a case. They also provide an official transcript that can be used in trial if a witness cannot attend or changes his or her account of an incident.

Affidavits

Affidavits are written sworn statements made by witnesses or parties to a case. They can be submitted at trial as official testimony if the witness in question does not attend in person.

Motions, Settlement, and Pre-Trial Conferences

A lot of things can happen before trial. Defense attorneys often try to get a lawsuit dismissed before it can go too far, or to have the trial moved to a more favorable court. Both sides often attempt to settle the matter early. If the case is proceeding, the attorneys for both parties must meet with the judge to discuss the lawsuit.

Motions

Most lawsuits involve a flurry of motions. A defendant can file a motion to dismiss the complaint, alleging that the plaintiff has failed to state a claim upon which relief can be granted (i.e., the plaintiff's claim is no good). A motion to dismiss a claim can also be based on the plaintiff's failure to follow all the required steps of the lawsuit. A motion for a change of venue requests that the case be transferred to a different court, one that may treat the defendant more favorably than the original one. A motion for summary judgment asks the court to rule in favor of one party or the other purely on the basis of the facts.

Settlement

Most cases never reach trial. Instead, the parties meet and come to an arrangement that satisfies both of them. Settling can save a lot of time and money. Unfortunately, the cost of defending a lawsuit is so great that many defendants who do not believe they are guilty agree to settle a lawsuit simply because it is cheaper than pursuing it to trial—and also because the results of trial can be quite unpredictable.

Pre-Trial Conference

Before trial occurs, both attorneys must meet with the judge who will preside over it. They discuss issues involved in the case, evidence, witnesses they will present, scheduling, and other such matters. (There should be nothing secret between opposing sides; trials are not won by surprise, but by the weight of the evidence and the persuasiveness of the arguments.) The case will then be placed on the court's calendar.

Trial

The big day finally arrives. The court is ready to hear the case. Attorneys for both sides have alerted parties and witnesses that they need to be ready to go to the courthouse on a certain day.

Jury Selection
If the trial is to involve a jury, the attorneys for both sides must choose the members of the jury panel. They don't actually choose specific jurors, but instead reject the ones they find unsuitable—usually the ones they suspect would lean toward the opposing side. Each side may strike the same number of jurors. Eventually a jury and an alternate or two are selected, and trial may begin.

Opening Statements
The plaintiff's attorney begins trial by explaining the facts of the case: why the plaintiff has sued, what injury the plaintiff has suffered, and what evidence the attorney will produce to prove that the plaintiff deserves some compensation. The defendant's attorney then makes an opening statement, which explains why the defendant should not be required to compensate the plaintiff.

Witnesses and Evidence
In the direct examination the plaintiff's attorney begins calling witnesses to the stand and asking them questions that are designed to prove his or her case. In the cross examination the defendant's attorney may then question the same witnesses. The plaintiff's attorney may also produce any exhibits of evidence that help prove his or her case. Once the plaintiff's attorney is done with this process, the defendant's attorney has a chance to do the same thing; now the plaintiff's attorney gets to cross-examine the witnesses for the defense.

Rebuttal
The plaintiff's attorney may now rebut any arguments made by the defense, calling witnesses and producing evidence as necessary. Then the defendant's attorney may rebut the plaintiff's rebuttal.

Closing Arguments
The plaintiff's attorney makes a speech summarizing the plaintiff's case, once again explaining why the plaintiff should prevail and asking the court to rule on the plaintiff's behalf. The defendant's attorney then summarizes his or her case. Finally, the plaintiff's attorney may rebut the defense's closing argument, so the plaintiff gets the last word.

Jury Charges
In a jury trial, the judge now reads a long list of instructions to the jury, explaining the law to them and describing how they should

apply it to particular facts. Sometimes jurors are given a written copy of these instructions; other times they are expected to listen carefully and remember them, though they may ask to hear them again during deliberation.

Deliberation

In a jury trial, the jury goes to a separate room to discuss how they should rule on the case. When they have reached their verdict, they return to the courtroom and inform the judge of their decision. In a bench trial, the judge or panel of judges decides how to rule.

Award of judgment

With verdict in hand, the judge now enters judgment for one party or the other, including any awards of damages. If the plaintiff has won, he or she may now try to collect damages, which is not always easy to do. In addition, the plaintiff's attorney usually takes a percentage of any winnings.

Appeal

If the losing party is unhappy with the court's decision, he or she has a set time in which to file an appeal. An appeal freezes the judgment issued by the trial court so neither party has to comply with it for the time being. Appeals can only be filed for a limited number of reasons, and the appeal process can take even longer than the initial lawsuit.

Statistics on Employment, Wages, and Profits

Attorneys

According to the U.S. Department of Labor, about 27 percent of lawyers are self-employed. That figure includes partners in law firms of all sizes as well as solo practitioners.

In 2006, there were about 761,000 lawyers working in the United States. This number does not include the relatively small number of people with law degrees who work as law professors, law school administrators, or judges.

The median income for all lawyers in 2007 was $106,120. The middle half of all lawyers earned between $72,060 and $145,600. That means 25 percent of lawyers earned more than the top amount, and 25 percent earned less than the lower amount. Salaries varied drastically by type of employment and amount of experience. In general, attorneys in private practice and in corporate legal departments have the highest incomes. Among government attorneys, those who work in the federal government make more than those in state and local governments.

Industry: Annual Mean Wage, May 2007	
Attorneys in corporations	$143,830
Private practice attorneys	$142,230
Federal government	$119,730
Local government	$87,130
State government	$78,310

Solo practitioners typically make less than partners in law firms. It can take several years to build up a viable solo practice, and it is not uncommon for solo practitioners to supplement their income with part-time jobs in other areas.

Salaries vary greatly by location. Attorneys in big cities with large legal markets make the highest salaries in the country. Attorneys in small towns in poor states tend to make much less, though their cost of living may be much lower.

Annual Mean Wage for Lawyers by Location	
Washington, D.C.	$143,520
California	$137,300
New York	$136,900
Delaware	$132,950
Georgia	$130,530

Starting salaries for new attorneys increased rapidly between 2004 and 2007. Some of the largest firms in big cities increased starting wages by $35,000 between those years, so that graduates starting practice in 2007 were receiving between $140,000 and $160,000 a year. These salaries are reserved for top graduates of top law schools; if you want this level of pay, you will need near-perfect grades and you will have to work in New York, Los Angeles, or one of the other large metropolitan areas that are home to the nation's biggest law firms. You will also have to be willing to work most of the time; firms that pay big salaries expect their attorneys to put in a lot of hours.

Though some attorneys do indeed earn princely sums, the vast majority does not. A median salary of slightly over $100,000 for experienced attorneys means that most lawyers can live comfortably, but remember that student loans can take a huge chunk of your income. The average debt for a law graduate in 2007 was about $85,000; even making six figures, it will take you a while to pay that off and reap the full benefits of a high income. The median salary for most new law school graduates is about $60,000. Those who work in firms may make slightly more, up to $85,000. Those who go to work in the government or who take on judicial clerkships make about $45,000. The median entry-level salary for a legal services attorney in 2008 was $40,000; this number increases to about $60,000 for legal services attorneys with 11–15 years of experience.

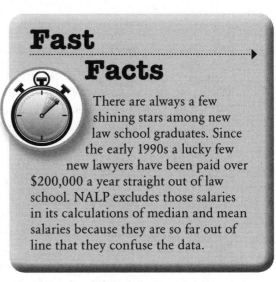

Fast Facts

There are always a few shining stars among new law school graduates. Since the early 1990s a lucky few new lawyers have been paid over $200,000 a year straight out of law school. NALP excludes those salaries in its calculations of median and mean salaries because they are so far out of line that they confuse the data.

When consulting statistics on salaries, it is important to remember the difference between the "median" and the "mean." The median is the halfway point; in other words, if the median entry-level salary is $60,000, then half of new attorneys make more than that and half make less. The mean is the average. The danger with confusing the median and the mean is that a few exceptionally high salaries can raise the mean well above the median, making it look as if most entry level attorneys make more than they do. In 2007, the mean salary for new lawyers was close to $80,000, but in fact the majority of new attorneys were making much less than that.

In 2007 the National Association for Law Placement (NALP) published a chart depicting the distribution of salaries in the class of 2006. This chart showed that salaries no longer fall into a bell curve, but rather in a sort of barbell shape with two peaks, one in the

$135,000 to $145,000 range, and another in the $30,000 to $50,000 range. This is the result of the practice among the nation's most prominent law firms of paying their new recruits very high salaries, while most legal employers continue to provide a more modest level of compensation. However, the economic decline of 2008 may have put a stop to the trend of skyrocketing salaries, as law firms began firing attorneys and slowing hiring.

Paralegals and Legal Assistants

There were about 238,000 paralegals and legal assistants working in the United States in 2006, with 70 percent employed at private law firms. Most of the rest worked for the government and for legal departments in corporations. A small percentage of paralegals work on their own, offering their services as freelancers.

In 2007, the median annual wage for paralegals and legal assistants was $44,990. The lowest-paid paralegals made about $28,360, while top earners made $71,000 or more. Pay depends more on a paralegal's experience and the location of his or her job than type of employer. Paralegals and legal assistants generally make between $40,000 and $60,000 in both private and government practice. The highest mean wages for paralegals are concentrated in the San Jose-San Francisco area, where the mean annual wage for legal assistants is between $61,000 and $66,000.

Annual Mean Wage for Legal Assistants by Location	
Washington, D.C.	$57,450
New York	$55,450
California	$54,570
Vermont	$53,740
Alaska	$52,310

Salaries for various other legal assistants, secretaries, and staffers are also competitive. Legal secretary salaries range between $30,000 and $70,000, depending on location and years of experience. Law librarians generally make between $38,000 and $70,000 per year. Finally, litigation technology specialists can earn between $85,000 and $115,000, depending on market and skills. Law firms often pay bonuses to those in paralegal and assistant positions.

Current Trends

In 2006, the U.S. Department of Labor predicted that job growth for lawyers would be about average, with a growth rate of about 11 percent, between 2006 and 2016, but that competition for jobs would be fierce. The economic difficulties that began in late 2008

On the Cutting

Edge

Hot Practice Areas

Although clients will always need all types of legal assistance, the ABA predicts that certain areas will be in particularly high demand. At the beginning of 2009, its hot areas were:

- Intellectual Property
- Immigration
- Labor and Employment
- Corporate Investigations, particularly white-collar crime
- Complex Litigation
- Global Warming, which is a sub-specialty of environmental law
- Family law, particularly in the area of reproductive technology
- Estate Planning and Elder Law
- Animal Law, especially anticruelty laws
- Alternative Dispute Resolution, especially mediation
- Libel, as people begin to sue bloggers for saying nasty things about them
- Foreclosures and bankruptcy
- Insurance coverage

What about the unfortunate specialties that are seeing less business? Mergers and acquisitions practice fell off in late 2008 as businesses started to collapse instead of buying one another. Structured finance was no longer popular after the subprime mortgage fiasco of 2008. Workers' compensation and medical malpractice cases were off as well.

may have changed that trend. As the economy tightened, the job market for new law graduates began to shrink and law firms began to lay off lawyers and staff members. Businesses stopped purchasing the legal services that have been the bread and butter of a number of major law firms, such as mergers and acquisitions work. Some major firms actually shut down completely. Graduates in 2008 and students expecting to graduate in 2009 were having a much harder time finding jobs than previous classes had. Almost 15,000 legal employees lost their jobs in 2008. A number of law firms and corporations stop hiring during recessions.

To add to the difficulties, lawyers are facing competition for legal jobs from paralegals and legal assistants and accounting firms. Paralegals can do almost all of the same work that attorneys do, and for a much lower price. Accounting firms can handle employee benefit issues and taxes, produce documents, and perform other types of jobs that lawyers also do, such as legal research. Many companies and individuals are now choosing to avoid litigation as a way of resolving disputes, instead using alternative dispute resolution such as arbitration or mediation.

Nevertheless, there is still a market for lawyers. The population of the United States is growing, which will result in more criminal and civil cases and transactions. Work in growing fields such as health care, bankruptcy, environmental law, energy law, elder law, and intellectual property will continue to be available. People will always need certain legal services, such as criminal defense, divorce, foreclosures, real estate closings, and help with trusts and estates, although demand for some of these services drops during recessions. The government will always need lawyers to man its many departments.

The trend in legal practice has been toward increased specialization, larger law firms, and an increasing number of staff attorneys who are not on partnership track and contract attorneys who are not even employees of the firms for which they work. It will become increasingly difficult for solo lawyers to develop their own practices. The need for specialization and the cost of resources such as research materials and insurance favor larger firms, as do the pro bono requirements imposed by most bars. Most law firm jobs are in cities, near government agencies and major corporations. Attorneys who want to start their own practices will do best in smaller towns and suburbs away from the law firms that inhabit urban areas.

The highest-paying jobs for lawyers will continue to go to the graduates of top-ranked law schools who receive the best grades while in law school. This has long been the case, but a tightening job market means that the competition for prime law firm spots and top judicial clerkships will be even keener. Law school graduates and attorneys who are willing to move for jobs will have an advantage over those who must stay where they are. Work experience will be a valuable credential, as will advanced law degrees in specialized areas such as tax or patent law. Multiple bar memberships can sometimes be an advantage, especially if an attorney wishes to move to another state.

An ever increasing number of attorneys are turning to temporary staffing agencies to find work for them. These agencies place attorneys in short-term jobs with firms and corporations that need temporary help. Much of this work involves massive document review projects. Some attorneys see contract document review work as a good way to build experience that can lead to full-time jobs. Some prefer this type of work to full-time work because it offers them flexibility that they would not have as an associate attorney at a firm. Others feel that it is a dead end that offers no hope for career advancement. Nevertheless, a number of attorneys find themselves forced to take this type of work because it is the only job available to them.

A number of attorneys and new graduates will not be able to find work within the legal field. Many attorneys work in banks, insurance companies, real estate companies, and other companies where they may or may not be able to put their legal training to good use. Accounting firms have a history of hiring law school graduates.

Employment of paralegals and legal assistants is growing much faster than that of lawyers, and in fact much faster than many other fields. The BLS predicted that employment for paralegals would grow 22 percent between 2006 and 2016. The job market for paralegals, like that for attorneys, has slowed down somewhat due to the poor economy that developed in 2008, but paralegals are less vulnerable to economic downturns than higher-paid lawyers. At the same time, a large number of people are entering the field, so competition is keen as well. The best jobs will go to paralegals with both training and experience, especially if they bring such specialty skills as nursing along with them.

The reason paralegals are so popular is that they can do nearly everything lawyers can, but at a fraction of the cost. Paralegals and legal assistants can draft documents, perform legal research, interview clients and witnesses, and do nearly any other legal task except actually represent a client and offer legal advice. As businesses try to reduce costs, they are using paralegals to perform tasks that might have once been done by lawyers.

Both law firms and corporation legal departments will be hiring paralegals. So will community legal service programs; federal, state, and local governments; courts; and consumer organizations.

Part-Time and Flexible Schedules

In 2008, only 5.6 percent of attorneys were working part-time; three quarters of them were women. Only two percent of male attorneys work part-time. Among female lawyers, about 12 percent of partners and 10 percent of associates are part-timers. Most law firms technically allow part-time schedules but few attorneys take advantage of them.

If you want a flexible schedule, go ahead and ask for it; chances are your employer will be willing to listen if you can explain how you can make the arrangement work. Take responsibility for getting your work done, be extra careful to communicate with all your co-workers, and understand that your advancement may be somewhat slower than it would be if you worked full-time.

Women and Minorities

The percentage of women and minorities working as attorneys at law firms has grown slowly since the early 1990s but these groups are still underrepresented, especially at the partnership level. As of 2008, women made up about half of law school graduates. About 45 percent of associates were female. Only about 19 percent of partners were female. Minorities accounted for about 19 percent of associates but only six percent of partners. Minority women show the lowest numbers, making up less than two percent of partners in major law firms. NALP concludes that these numbers mean that law firms are doing a good job of recruiting women and minorities to summer associate and associate positions, but that these individuals are leaving their jobs at a higher rate than men and non-minorities. These has been much talk about improving retention among these groups, but so far changes have been slow.

Retiring Baby Boomers

A large percentage of senior partners and upper-level corporate and government counsel are starting to reach retirement age. While this may mean that younger attorneys will have an opportunity to move into those gaps, it is also likely to affect the viability of a number of firms and practices. Older attorneys have clients and contacts who rely on them personally, perhaps as the result of several decades of legal work. When those attorneys retire, their clients may take their business elsewhere. Some law firms have responded to this demographic phenomenon by trying to include more attorneys in client relationships. They are teaming older attorneys with younger ones and encouraging the older lawyers to teach the younger ones what they know, so that the clients begin to see their relationships as being with the entire firm instead of just with individual attorneys.

Unhappy Lawyers

For many years, lawyers as a group have been among the unhappiest professionals in the United States. About 20 percent of lawyers suffer depression during their careers. Most firms lose about 20 percent of their associates every year. A survey done by the American Bar Association revealed that 44 percent of current lawyers would not recommend that a young person enter the profession.

Why are lawyers so unhappy? The biggest reason seems to be the long hours that many work. The requirement to bill a certain number of hours every year forces attorneys to spend 60 hours a week or more on the job, with little time for vacation or a personal life. Add to that work that can sometimes be boring or tedious, competition with fellow lawyers for assignments and promotions, and the declining prestige of the legal profession, and you have a recipe for dissatisfaction.

This does not mean all lawyers are unhappy. Many attorneys love what they do. They enjoy the mental challenge, the thrill of arguing cases, and the satisfaction of a job well done. In-house lawyers, legal services lawyers, and lawyers who work for the government often like their work more than their peers in law firms.

Possible Future Trends

Competition

Within the United States, the supply of lawyers is more than sufficient to meet the needs of the public. Top-ranked firms and top-ranked graduates of law schools still manage to find ample clients; the rest of the nation's attorneys have a harder time making ends meet. Small and mid-sized firms find themselves operating in a buyer's market, in which customers have their choice of attorneys. This forces some attorneys to set their rates according to their clients' wishes, and prevents them from making as much money as they might like. It also means that lawyers and law firms must constantly compete for business from corporations and individuals.

The conclusions are simple enough. Young attorneys will find stiff competition for jobs. Paralegals and other staffers will have an easier time finding work, though competition for them will be stiff as well.

Outsourcing

Although the legal profession has been slow to embrace the outsourcing trend, law firms and corporate law offices are gradually starting to consider sending their work overseas. Lawyers in India and some other countries with good English speakers can do research and writing and some other types of work for less than half the price charged by American lawyers. There are now a number of international companies that will outsource legal research for United States attorneys and other clients. Labor-intensive projects such as document review and due diligence-the practice of examining a company's or institution's actions to see if it complies with all applicable laws, rules, and regulations—also find their way overseas.

Within the United States, a growing number of firms and individual lawyers are offering similar services. Some lawyers specialize in legal research and writing, or appellate brief writing. They sell their services to other lawyers who do not have the time to write lengthy pieces. Other firms employ paralegals to provide legal consulting services to clients, often over the Internet. All these types of services compete with "traditional" law firms by performing the same tasks for less money. On the other hand, the attorneys and paralegals who choose to provide outsourced services may find that they have ample business.

Billing Trends and Law Firms

Some observers of the legal field have suggested that big law firms are soon to be a thing of the past. The argument goes that law firms traditionally served as one-stop shops offering clients a range of legal services under one roof, similar to a department store. If a person needed a legal expert, the best way to find one was to contact a law firm. This convenience came at the cost of efficiency, as firms had to support all their attorneys, even the ones who were not accomplishing much.

The Internet has made that business model unnecessary. Now a client can do a quick search and find any number of attorneys who can do whatever work is necessary. This should provide an

Problem
Solving

Does Law School Need to Be Three Years Long?

This is a very real question among many law schools, students, and recent graduates. Critics of the third year argue that students do not learn much and spend a lot of their time goofing off. They contend that students would be better off diving straight into the practice of law, which is where they learn the essential skills of the profession anyway. Third year is ostensibly a way for law schools to make more money.

Supporters of the third year counter that law is so complicated that students need that extra year of specialty classes. Third year gives students an opportunity to participate in clinics, seminars, and other activities that give them a solid grounding in the field. In addition, the recruiting calendar is set up around a three-year schedule, and many students use summers to earn money to pay tuition. The ABA has no intention of allowing law schools to shorten their curricula, and most law schools seem quite happy to run things the way they are. Some schools, though, have begun setting up alternative schedules. The University of Dayton, for example, now offers a two-year law degree that includes two summers of study—same tuition but one year less living expenses. Northwestern University also offers an accelerated JD that can be completed in five semesters arranged to allow students to work at law firms during one summer just like their more traditional peers. More schools may follow suit.

opportunity for small firms and solo practitioners to come to the attention of clients who in the past would have overlooked them because they assumed they had to hire a law firm.

Law firms ostensibly are not interested in efficiency because their profits depend on growth, both in numbers and in hourly rates. A growing number of clients of law firms, both private businesses and corporate general counsels, are protesting against hourly billing. They complain that in billing by the hour, lawyers are selling time, but what their customers want to buy is results. Corporate clients particularly complain about the high rates they pay for inexperienced junior attorneys.

Salary Freezes and Merit-Based Bonuses

In late 2008 and early 2009 a number of law firms announced some shocking news: they would not be increasing salaries for associates that year. Profits for many law firms fell in 2008, leading partners to reconsider their practice of raising salaries in lockstep with other firms every year. Some of the same firms also announced that bonuses would no longer be based on the number of hours billed, but instead would be based on merit. Some associates protested; others were just thankful that they had not been fired.

A number of law firms are thinking about ways to increase their efficiency and lower their cost to clients. In order to do this, they will probably increase the number of non-lawyers working for them (mainly paralegals), reduce the number of associates working toward partnership, and increase the number of staff attorneys.

Working Overseas

What does a young lawyer with no job in the United States do? Fly overseas! Secretaries, paralegals, and other support staff are welcome, too. In 2008, hundreds of young lawyers took jobs in foreign countries. Dubai was especially popular, and reputed to be lucrative. Doha and Riyadh were starting to hire more attorneys as of late 2008. China, Hong Kong, and Spain also attracted large numbers of American lawyers. American attorneys have even found jobs in Micronesia. Attorneys who take these jobs do not necessarily need to be admitted to any state bar.

Young attorneys look at these jobs as a way of gaining experience that will help them market themselves when they return home.

Some experienced attorneys have moved overseas as well. The pay is attractive, and Americans working abroad sometimes escape paying U.S. income taxes.

Important Technology

LexisNexis and Westlaw

LexisNexis, popularly called Lexis, and Westlaw are the granddaddies of electronic legal databases. Each of them offers a searchable database of court decisions and statutes, law reviews, court orders, and other primary sources. They can also provide CLE (continuing legal education courses), integrated litigation workflow tools, assistance with research and document drafting, and other services. A subscription to Westlaw or Lexis can actually replace a physical law library, and an increasing number of lawyers and paralegals do all their research online with one of these services. The catch? Both of these services are expensive. They offer different pricing schemes to meet the needs of different practitioners, and lawyers do try to pass the cost along to clients, but they can still be quite pricey.

Best Practice

Employers often will mention specific software packages in job advertisements. They may express their desire that a new associate or paralegal be proficient at Ringtail, for example. If you are still in law school or studying to be a paralegal, look through job advertisements on Monster.com and other Web sites and see which programs are desirable—then learn how to use them!

Martindale-Hubbell

Martindale-Hubbell, found at http://martindale.com, is the premier national directory of lawyers and law firms. Listings are searchable by location, practice area, law school, languages spoken, and other categories. Martindale.com) also offers information on professional associations, continuing legal education, experts, careers, and other areas. Martindale is a great resource for finding potential employers or professional assistance. For example, say you work in Tennessee.

A client asks you whether he needs a contractor's license in order to do some construction work in Alabama. You could spend hours researching Alabama law, about which you know nothing, or you could do a quick search on Martindale to find an Alabama attorney who specializes in construction law and get your question answered right away.

Blogs

In the past few years lawyers have started using blogs as a way to build their practices and showcase their areas of expertise. Some blogs contain basic information for non-lawyers. Some track the most recent cases and explain developments in particular areas of the law. Whatever legal job you take, keeping a blog can be a good way to attract clients. If your employer does not have a blog, why not volunteer to start one?

E-Discovery and Litigation Support

Electronic discovery, the process of locating and examining electronic data for possible use as evidence in a legal case, is a growing field. It is still quite new, and not all lawyers have gotten on board with the practice. The information technology professionals at law firms and other law offices are still figuring out how to integrate e-discovery packages with their existing software systems. The trend is obvious, though; experts predict that total spending on e-discovery will be close to five billion dollars by 2011. Lawyers, paralegals, and other staffers who can use e-discovery software will be in high demand.

The practice of e-discovery is not yet solidified. A number of software companies have begun producing packages to handle e-discovery and provide litigation support. These packages typically help lawyers organize and review documents and assemble them for trial. Popular programs include CT Summation, Concordance, and Ringtail by FTI. Kazeon Systems sells e-discovery software used to collect, organize, and store documents for legal or regulatory proceedings. Other e-discovery software vendors include i365, Autonomy, and AXS-One. E-discovery packages are extremely expensive. In early 2009, for example, Kazeon offered a perpetual license to use its software for about $80,000. For clients who didn't want to pay

On the Cutting Edge

Cameras and Digital Animation

If you end up doing litigation, you may well find yourself taking photographs. Images of accident locations, vehicles, buildings with crumbling plaster, and gruesome injuries can all play a part in court cases. Sometimes videos can provide useful information to a jury. Skill with a camera-either still or video-can translate into legal job opportunities. Digital cameras and photo editing software improve every year, but they cannot replace actual skill at taking images.

Gone are the days when juries sat passively listening to attorneys describe events verbally, perhaps with the aid of a poster. Now jurors expect to see animated images of exactly what happened in the car accident or murder, or whatever else they are being expected to judge. If you can learn how to make trial animations, you can find good work as a litigation technology specialist, whether you are an attorney, paralegal, or computer person.

that much up front, it sold a license to start a case for $10,000 and then sold storage space for between $100 and $150 per gigabyte.

Major Players and Industry Forces

The law profession regulates itself through state bar associations. They impose strict admission requirements on new lawyers and take disciplinary action against lawyers who do not act in accordance with ethical standards.

Scholars of the legal field note that it is important for the profession to remain independent from the government. Self-governing lawyers are not dependent on the government for the right to practice, which makes it easier for lawyers to challenge governmental practices that they find unjust or illegal.

Although state bar associations play the central role in regulating the profession, there are also national organizations of attorneys, paralegals, and legal secretaries. All of these groups sponsor conferences at the national, regional, and state levels. Which conferences will be important to a practitioner depend on his or her specialty; state bar conferences in particular are well-attended and popular with attorneys.

State Bars

In order to practice law in a state, you must be a member of its bar. A "bar" is a self-governing organization that manages the legal profession within a geographic area. State supreme courts play a key role in overseeing the bar; these courts administer oaths of office, admit new attorneys to practice, and discipline attorneys found guilty of infractions.

In order to ensure that all attorneys practicing law within a state are qualified, the state bar requires all prospective lawyers to meet several criteria. These vary, but they can include:

➡ Graduating from an accredited law school or otherwise having fulfilled an approved training program
➡ Passing the state's bar exam
➡ Passing the Multistate Professional Responsibility Examination (MPRE)
➡ Undergoing a background check to ensure that the prospective attorney is someone of "good moral character"
➡ Completing a transitional program that introduces beginning lawyers to the practice of law and/or introduces all new lawyers (recent graduates and those transferring from other states) to the law practice in that state
➡ Paying dues
➡ Swearing an oath

Some states admit attorneys who have practiced for several years in other states as long as they meet certain criteria. This is known as "reciprocity." Not all state bars have reciprocal agreements with other state bars. If an attorney cannot join another state's bar through reciprocity, then he or she must take the other state's bar exam and fulfill the other requirements of bar membership. Once an attorney is admitted, he or she receives a state bar number. Attorneys include this number with their signatures when they sign documents to be submitted to courts.

State bars run education programs throughout the year. These are known as Continuing Legal Education, or CLE. There are CLEs available on almost every legal topic, from insurance to mechanics' liens to the intricacies of income tax. Often state attorneys will put on the programs themselves; teaching a CLE is seen as a good way to make contacts and find clients as well as to improve one's knowledge of the law. Most states require bar members to attend a certain number of hours of CLE every year to ensure that they are keeping up with developments in the law and adding to their skills.

Bar associations handle the discipline of attorneys within the state. If an attorney is accused of misconduct by a client or a fellow attorney, the bar will investigate the incident. If the attorney has indeed committed an ethics violation, the bar can administer various punishments. These include warnings, probation, and temporary suspension from the practice of law. An attorney who commits a truly grievous offense can be disbarred, meaning he or she is no longer an attorney within that state and cannot practice law anymore.

State bar associations perform a number of other services for members and the general public. They offer resources on practicing in the state, such as reference materials and magazines. They usually publish newsletters that may include interpretations of recent court rulings, articles on topics of interest to lawyers within the state, and advertisements for jobs. Members of the general public can consult state bars for legal information or to find a lawyer.

Most bars organize various specialty groups, such as for young lawyers, litigators, corporate practitioners, or construction lawyers. These groups may sponsor community outreach projects, educational conferences, and social events. Many lawyers especially enjoy attending these events because they are an opportunity to talk shop with colleagues and make professional connections.

American Bar Association (ABA)

The American Bar Association is an organization of attorneys and law students throughout the United States. It has over 400,000 members, around half of all lawyers in the country. Membership is voluntary, and many lawyers do not belong to the ABA. The ABA's two biggest roles within the American legal profession are setting

INTERVIEW

Opportunities in the Industry

Laura Kissel
Associate, Gibbs & Bruns LLP

How long have you practiced law? What kind of law do you practice?

I have practiced law since the fall of 2004, so I am into my fifth year! Seems very hard to believe at times. The law firm I work for is referred to as a litigation boutique that only practices commercial civil litigation. I have heard partners at the firm describe our practice as "complex commercial litigation" as well. The actual types of cases that I have worked on have varied: securities litigation, shareholder derivative lawsuits, partnership disputes, general commercial disputes, construction disputes, employment related litigation, litigation involving a charitable trust, defending a law firm in a malpractice case, representing parties involved in corporate buyout disputes, and patent infringement. I like the variety in the firm's practice because each new case allows you to learn a different area or facet of the law.

What sort of opportunities are there in the law? What types of jobs did your classmates take when they graduated from law school? Did anyone have trouble finding a job?

I did not know too many people who had real difficulty finding a job after law school (although the prognosis may be worse now than in 2004). A few of my friends took judicial clerkships right out of law school. Most of my friends ended up going to practice at law firms of some sort—some at the larger firms, such as Vinson & Elkins and Baker Botts with hundreds of lawyers and dozens of practice sections, some at smaller offices of large firms that are based in other cities, a few at very small specialized firms (one, for example, works for a small firm who does insurance law), and a few at litigation boutiques like Gibbs & Bruns.

That being said, I also know a handful of people who took non-firm jobs out of law school. A friend of mine took a job in the Texas Attorney General's office. Another friend works for a non-profit entity that represents (and assists other attorneys who represent) defendants in capital cases or death row inmates. I know other people who took jobs as prosecutors. I can't think of anyone who went to work in-house right out of law school, but I do know a few who took in-house jobs in their first couple of years. I also know a couple of people who went to work for legal recruiting firms after a few years practicing at firms.

Even though I went to school at U.T., I know people who went to work all over the United States—New York City, Denver, Washington, D.C, Atlanta, San Francisco, L.A.—and even one who went to work for a U.S.-based firm in London.

If you were not practicing at a law firm, what sort of legal job would you want instead?

I would probably work for a jury research/consulting firm. We used one in one of the first cases I worked on, and it really seemed like an interesting facet of the practice of law. People fascinate me—which is probably why I decided on an undergraduate psychology degree!—and studying the dynamics of the people and personalities on juries would be something I think I would really enjoy. Now I just need to get some actual trial experience under my belt, so that I could actually be of use in the area!

What about non-lawyers; what sort of opportunities do you know of for paralegals, trial technology specialists, etc?

I am a firm believer that you are only as good as your support team. Especially in the large-scale cases that our firm takes, it honestly takes a whole team of people to get the case ready to go to trial. I would not be sane most of the time if it were not for my legal secretary! The other essential members of the teams I work on are, as you mention, paralegals. We also frequently use trial technology specialists for trials, arbitrations, or major hearings to manage the electronic presentation of exhibits, create elaborate PowerPoint presentations, develop fancy, demonstrative visual exhibits for the jury or the court.

Do you think the economic downturn of 2008-09 will hurt the legal profession as a whole?

I am sure that it will affect some sections of the practice of law. Corporate lawyers may have less work because there are less business deals being done, for example. It is hard to say how it will affect litigation firms like Gibbs & Bruns. I personally have been just as busy (actually even busier) in 2008 and the first part of 2009 than years before. However that may be a function of the fact that our firm has 20 plus partners and only eight associates!

I do know that the larger law firms (both in Texas and in major metropolitan areas like New York City) are hiring fewer new associates than they did in the past. *(continued on next page)*

INTERVIEW

Opportunities in the Industry (continued)

What tips would you give a person contemplating a career in the law? What about someone soon to graduate from law school?

I would tell a person who is thinking about becoming a lawyer to make sure that it is something that they truly want to do before they commit the time, effort, and money to getting a law degree. Law school is a really challenging (and rewarding) experience, but I knew several classmates who really did not have the desire to study or practice the law, and they struggled. I have wanted to be a lawyer since my parents let me stay up late when I was little to watch *L.A. Law* on TV. Once I made it to high school, however, my parents encouraged me to talk to people who were in the field to see if it was really what I wanted as a long-term career. I was fortunate (I lived in a small town) that I was able to work for a sole practitioner and in the county district court to really get a flavor for what being a lawyer means on a day-to-day basis. I saw both the good and the bad but was still determined to go to law school. In college I worked as a runner and legal secretary for a small firm in Kansas City-and got to see some different aspects of the practice of law. Therefore, when

ethics standards and approving law schools. The organization also publishes a number of books and periodicals, sponsors educational seminars and conferences, rates lawyers nominated for judgeships (e.g., the ABA will announce that it believes a given nominee is qualified, well qualified, or not qualified to be a federal judge), and publishes statements on the legality of certain actions, such as the president's interpretation of Constitutional rules.

An ABA-accredited law school is a law school that the ABA judges worthy of its approval. The vast majority of state bars will admit graduates only of ABA-accredited law schools. (California and New York are two exceptions.) Graduates of non-accredited law schools need not apply. This rule may be changing, though. In the fall of 2008, the Supreme Court of Massachusetts ruled that a graduate of an online law school who was already a member of the California

I graduated college I was as certain as a 22 year old can be that I would enjoy being a lawyer. I wouldn't say that I knew exactly what I was getting myself into, but I had a good frame of reference for the skills, hard work, dedication, and drive that a career in the law would entail.

I would tell someone soon to graduate from law school to not get discouraged when they inevitably feel like they don't know a single thing about the law and don't have a clue what it means to "practice" law. Now that I have a few years behind me, I can see that law school (at least the law school I attended) did not teach me how to be a lawyer on a day-to-day basis. There is no class on how to "practice" law. What law school does is teach you the skills and ways of thinking to make you a good lawyer. Translating that knowledge into a rewarding legal career is something that takes time and trial and error to a certain extent. You only learn by doing, and you will learn something new every day that you practice. I would also tell them that probably the most challenging thing about being a lawyer is dealing with clients. I don't mean that in a bad way, it is just one area of the practice that I had never thought about in law school. Clients can be difficult or super appreciative, scared or overeager. They may second-guess every decision you make or they may call you at all hours asking for your take on various issues. Having the patience to navigate clients through litigation takes another set of skills that they don't teach you in law school. Be sure you listen to your clients and are attentive to their needs and requests, and you will do just fine!

state bar would be allowed to take the Massachusetts bar exam. Around that time, the ABA announced that it would begin a comprehensive review of its approval standards for law schools, which may result in more degrees from online or correspondence institutions being accepted for bar applications.

The American Bar Association (ABA) holds an annual meeting for its members. Participants can attend seminars on legal topics, listen to speeches, and meet one another at parties and social gatherings.

Paralegal Associations

The National Association of Legal Assistants is a professional association for paralegals and legal assistants. With about 18,000 members in the United States, the group provides training and continuing education for paralegals, including certification programs. It works to achieve recognition of the legal assistant profession, set professional standards, track legislation concerning legal assistants, and research the growth of the profession. Members receive a quarterly journal and access to NALA's online networking service.

The Certified Legal Assistant, or CLA, program was the first legal credentialing program for paralegals instituted in the United States. The CLA certification is recognized throughout the country. In 2004 NALA introduced an alternative credential, Certified Paralegal, or CP. In order to receive either the CLA or CP certification, applicants must pass an examination. Before a person can take the exam, he or she must either complete a legal assistant training program or earn a bachelor's degree and work for one year as a legal assistant. Individuals with a high school diploma and seven years' work experience also qualify for the test. The test measures an applicant's knowledge of legal research, legal terminology, ethics, communications, and substantive areas of the law such as contracts, family law, bankruptcy, or real estate. In 2006 NALA introduced a new advanced paralegal certification program available online.

The American Alliance of Paralegals, Inc., offers a certification called the American Alliance Certified Paralegal (AACP), which is available to paralegals with at least five years' experience and certain types of training. AACP holders must take a set number of hours of CLE every year.

The National Federation of Paralegal Associations was founded in 1974 and claims to be the first national paralegal association in the United States. Membership includes over 11,000 individual paralegals and more than 50 paralegal associations throughout the country. NFPA is particularly interested in monitoring legislative news that affects legal assistants, representing paralegals' interests within the legal profession, and helping the paralegal profession transition into a new form of legal practice. It offers CLEs for paralegals, courses in professional development, and assistance in networking and finding jobs.

NFPA offers the Registered Paralegal (RP) certification to paralegals who have two years' experience and a bachelor's degree, and who pass an examination called PACE (Paralegal Advanced Competency Exam). PACE tests a paralegal's knowledge of general law, ethics, and specialized areas of the law. Those who hold the RP certification must also complete CLE regularly.

Problem
Solving

Did Juror Influence Defendant's Decision?

Imagine you're a lawyer representing a major automobile manufacturer. You have spent several days at trial, defending your company against a lawsuit brought by a woman who was paralyzed from the neck down when one of your vehicles rolled over. Testimony has ended, and the jury has been deliberating for several hours when a note comes out of the jury room. The judge reads it: "What is the maximum amount that can be awarded?" What would you do?

What the actual lawyers in this case did was quickly settle for $3 million. They assumed that the question meant the jury had already found the company liable and were now trying to decide on the amount of damages. The company probably thought $3 million was less than the jury would award. Alas for the company and its lawyers, when the attorneys went to discuss the case with the jurors, it turned out that the jurors had been leaning toward the car company—11 to one. The note had come from the single holdout juror, and she had sent it to the judge over the objections of her fellow jurors.

Since then the car company has refused to pay the settlement amount and has asked the court to void the settlement. The lawyers claim that they were the victims of jury misconduct, and that the settlement was the result of fraud. So far the courts have refused to grant the company's request and the trial judge has ordered the company to pay. And the victim? Since the 2002 accident, she has lived in a nursing home, supported by Medicaid.

The National Association for Legal Professionals offers a certification called Professional Paralegal (PP) to paralegals who pass a four-part exam.

National Association of Legal Secretaries (NALS)

NALS now refers to itself as the "association for legal professionals" as a way of opening membership from simply legal secretaries to paralegals and other legal service workers. NALS has chapters and associations at both the state and local level and holds regional and national conferences every year. Members receive discounts on legal education, publications, and other services, a subscription to a magazine, and access to the organization's online learning center. Legal secretaries seeking certification can acquire one of two credentials: Accredited Legal Secretary (ALS) for secretaries with one year of experience, and Professional Legal Secretary (PLS) for those with three years experience. Both certification programs require applicants to pass an examination. The exams cover office skills, ethics, and judgment, procedural law, legal research, and the preparation of legal documents.

Chapter 3

On the Job

The legal profession employs thousands of people. Though the field is immense and offers a huge variety of work, in one sense there are only two main types of jobs: attorneys and paralegals. The attorneys do the official legal work, and the paralegals, or legal assistants, help them.

To keep a legal practice running, though, requires the work of many more staff people. Legal secretaries prepare and organize documents, set schedules, communicate with clients, and do a multitude of other essential tasks. Legal staffers handle human resources, run law libraries, perform e-discovery, prepare electronic exhibits for trials, and take care of all the other aspects of running a business.

Attorneys may work in law firms, on their own, in corporate legal departments, or in the government. Legal practices are usually divided into two types, private and public or governmental. Most private practice attorneys work in law firms; a minority are employed by corporations. Government lawyers work for cities, states, the federal government, or other public entities. Some legal professionals end up in classrooms or courtrooms as professors or judges.

The lists in this chapter are divided into types of law, types of legal practice and the jobs within them, and legal staff jobs. Types of law and types of legal practice will overlap. For example, you may become an associate in a law firm and a specialist in mergers and acquisitions. Or you may go work for the government as a staff attorney specializing in tax law. Few attorneys refer to themselves as just "attorneys." Instead, a person will call himself or herself a real estate lawyer or litigator or public defender. Specialty and type of practice combined give a person's real job title.

Though much of this chapter focuses on positions for attorneys, almost all of the information applies as well to paralegals, secretaries, and other legal support personnel. Staff members also work in either private or public practice, for associates or partners or general counsels, and specialize in just a few areas of the law.

Types of Law

An attorney, also known as a lawyer or an attorney-at-law, is a person who has graduated from law school and become licensed by a state to represent clients in legal matters. Attorneys give legal advice, file lawsuits and pleadings with courts, argue cases before judges and juries, draft legal documents such as contracts and wills, and perform real estate closings and many other tasks. But the actual work done by individual attorneys varies greatly by specialization and employer.

Most lawyers specialize in either litigation or transactional work. Litigators argue cases in court. Transactional lawyers do most of their work in offices. Do you like to stand up in front of people and talk extemporaneously? Then you will like litigation. Do you prefer to work behind the scenes, researching and writing and grappling with difficult legal concepts? Then you might prefer transactional work. Law comes in many varieties. If you become a lawyer or paralegal or work in a legal job, most likely you will specialize in just a few fields of law. Law firms arrange their practice groups around these legal fields. This list includes some of the most common legal fields in the United States.

Administrative

Administrative law, or regulatory law, is the body of laws, rules, and regulations created by federal and state government agencies to define exactly what those agencies are allowed to do. Agencies are organizations created by statutes to handle particular aspects of government work. U.S. federal agencies include the Central Intelligence

Agency, the Environmental Protection Agency, the National Science Foundation, the Securities and Exchange Commission, and many others. Agencies make and enforce rules that have the power of law in some cases.

Admiralty

Admiralty law, or maritime law, governs ships on the oceans. It includes navigation, commerce, shipping, piers and docks, canals, and even piracy. Attorneys who live in coastal areas near major ports may specialize in admiralty law.

Alternative Dispute Resolution

Alternative dispute resolution is settling conflicts by means other than litigation, such as conciliation, mediation, or arbitration. Litigation can be a very slow and inefficient (not to mention expensive) way to solve problems. For that reason, more and more states are encouraging the use of alternative dispute resolution, or ADR, which can end a conflict much more quickly than bringing it to trial. Many employment contracts, sales contracts, and international agreements now require people to try ADR before suing. An attorney who gets certified as an arbitrator or mediator can often find plentiful work in this area.

Appellate

Attorneys who specialize in appellate practice spend their time appealing court decisions to appeals courts. Appeals courts consider questions of law, unlike trial courts, which consider facts. To bring an appeal, an attorney must argue that the lower court made a mistake in the way it applied the law to the facts of the case. Arguments in appellate courts are made largely in writing. Attorneys write carefully argued briefs in which they state the questions they would like addressed and present legal arguments for their side. Most appeals courts do not permit oral arguments for most cases, so the appellate brief is the only way to win. Appellate practice tends to attract intellectual attorneys who especially enjoy exploring the intricacies of the law; if you enjoy being on the editorial board of a law review or legal journal, you may like appellate work.

Bankruptcy

Bankruptcy is the declaration by an individual or a company that it is unable to pay its debts. Attorneys who specialize in bankruptcy help their clients choose which type of bankruptcy is most appropriate (Chapter 7, Chapter 11, and Chapter 13 are the most common because they are the types used for individuals and corporations; there are three other less common types of bankruptcy) and file the cases with the bankruptcy court. They then help their clients liquidate their property, distribute the proceeds to creditors, and arrange for outstanding debts to be discharged.

Business

Business law is a big area, including corporations, mergers and acquisitions, secured transactions, commercial paper, securities regulation, corporate finance, bankruptcy, accounting, tax, venture capital, and general deal-making. There are lawyers who specialize in all these areas; some work with small businesses, some work with large companies, and some firms exist solely to do the work of one giant corporation.

Civil Law

Civil law actually has two different meanings. In one sense, it is the practice of law that involves private citizens and companies as opposed to criminal law, in which the government brings charges against accused criminals. When attorneys say that they work in civil law, that is often what they mean. Civil law can also refer to a legal system based on a code of created laws as opposed to common law, which is derived from court decisions based on specific cases. France, for example, bases its legal system on a code of laws created by experts. The United States is mainly a common law country. Louisiana uses both a civil code and common law.

Class Action

In a class action lawsuit plaintiffs form a group to bring a common claim to court, often when they have suffered the same type of injury from the same cause. Generally the injury is caused by a business or product, such as asbestos. Asbestos litigation has involved nearly one million plaintiffs. The class of plaintiffs forms because while each individual plaintiff may find it difficult or impossible to sue a corporation, a large group can succeed. In addition, in many cases the harm done to each plaintiff is outweighed by the cost of bringing a lawsuit, but when the injuries done to many people are combined it becomes much more efficient to bring a lawsuit and then divide the resulting compensation. Both plaintiffs' attorneys and defense attorneys can work with class action lawsuits. Some plaintiffs' attorneys specialize in class action lawsuits, which can be extremely profitable to law firms.

Contracts

Contract law is not exactly its own practice area; contracts appear in almost every area of the law. Still, not every attorney likes to write or read contracts. It is painstaking work that requires great attention to detail, so many firms have attorneys who specialize in drafting and reviewing contracts. A contract can constitute the entire legal agreement between parties in an area, so it is very important that every word is correct and appropriate; otherwise a person might discover too late that he has taken on a responsibility he did not expect.

Constitutional

The U.S. Constitution sets up the structure of the U.S. government and specifies a number of civil rights and civil liberties. Specialists in Constitutional law spend hours pondering the exact meaning and implications of the document when applied to daily life, in areas ranging from voting rights to affirmative action to sexual privacy. Strict constructionists try to find the exact meaning of the exact words used; liberal constructionists prefer to interpret meanings with more flexibility. The Supreme Court is the ultimate interpreter of the Constitution, and its interpretation changes as the years go by and as its composition fluctuates from liberal to conservative and back again.

Construction

Anyone who wants to build a building or other structure must follow numerous laws that regulate construction. Practitioners of construction law help builders and their clients through the complicated and lengthy process of designing a project, drafting a contract that avoids liability, handling the dispute resolution if things go wrong, filing mechanics' liens, researching contractors' licensing requirements, and dealing with any other aspect of the construction process that lends itself to legal assistance.

Criminal

If you want to work with lots of clients and spend time in court, criminal practice may be right for you. Criminal law deals with crime and maintaining law and order. Criminal lawyers include prosecutors, who bring cases against suspected criminals on behalf of the state; criminal defense lawyers, who defend people who are accused of crimes; and public defenders, who are paid by the state to defend suspected criminals at trial. Suspected criminals are welcome to pay for their own defense if they can afford it, and many do hire private defense attorneys. Public defenders exist to ensure that all those accused of crimes have legal representation in court. Students of criminal law learn the definitions of crimes, the mental states necessary to commit criminal acts, and the punishments that are appropriate for particular crimes.

Cyber Law

Cyber law is a new area that focuses on information technology and computers. Attorneys in this field handle matters related to intellectual property, freedom of speech, privacy, and other issues arising with the growth of the Internet. One challenge in this field is determining jurisdiction, i.e. which laws should apply to a given matter. Ordinarily jurisdiction is determined by physical location, but the Internet is everywhere at once.

Document Review

Document review is the process of examining the documents presented by the opposing party in a lawsuit in order to find those that are relevant to the case. In large-scale litigation, the parties may present so many documents that it takes large teams of attorneys and paralegals weeks to go through them all. Some attorneys, paralegals, and law school graduates spend all of their time working on projects of this sort. They may go to a particular location to look through boxes of paper documents. They may also do their work remotely on a computer, using programs such as Ringtail. Legal staffing agencies specialize in providing contract attorneys and paralegals for document reviews.

Domestic Relations/Family

Family law encompasses marriage, pre-nuptial agreements, separation, divorce, division of marital property, the custody and support of children, visitation, adoption, grandparents' rights, child abuse, and anything else related to the family. Family courts often work closely with social services systems and guardians ad litem, monitoring the well-being of children in less-than-ideal family arrangements. Family practice can be very gratifying but also depressing at times because so many of the clients are unhappy.

Employment

Employment law covers almost all aspects of working life except for labor unions and collective bargaining, which are considered labor law. Worker's compensation, discrimination, sexual harassment, salaries and wages, hiring and firing, unemployment compensation, pensions, benefits, and workplace safety all fall under the heading of employment law. There is a huge body of statutory material regulating employer-employee relationships and workplace issues, and an equally huge body of case law that increases every year as employees sue their employers for various grievances.

Entertainment

Entertainment lawyers work in the entertainment industry, which includes film and television, music, radio, theatre, visual arts, and publishing. They negotiate contracts and talent agreements, arrange for licenses, handle trade union issues, and help arrange for distribution of products such as films or video games. They handle intellectual property matters such as copyright infringement and accusations of defamation. Entertainment lawyers need to be very good at contract law and negotiation. This is a good field for someone who wants to live in New York or Los Angeles; though there are opportunities throughout the country, they are much thinner on the ground outside those big cities.

Environmental

Environmental law is governed by the Environmental Protection Agency and a number of federal statutes, which exist to protect the environment from public and private acts that can harm it. These include statutes against pollution of the air and water and statutes protecting endangered species. There is always tension between those who want to protect the environment and those who think that environmental protection comes at the cost of property rights, and environmental law attorneys can be found on either side of that divide. Environmental law is not just for tree huggers!

Health

Health law is the body of laws that regulates the health care industry. These days the legal issues surrounding health insurance are immense. Health law attorneys work with patients, doctors, vendors of medical and pharmaceutical products, and insurers. Their work may involve Medicare and Medicaid, workers' compensation laws, denial of coverage, children's health, reproductive rights, disparities in health care, prescription drug coverage, and any number of other areas. Attorneys in this field must keep up with the constantly changing array of health care laws.

Immigration

Immigration lawyers work with immigrants and would-be immigrants, filing forms with the INS, checking visa requirements, coming up with justifications to allow their clients to enter the country. They help immigrants with the naturalization process and assist them in their efforts to bring family members to this country. Speaking a foreign language or two can be an asset in this field.

Insurance Defense

Insurance defense attorneys defend insurance companies from claims including products liability, medical malpractice, negligence, property damage, and others. Insurance defense lawyers are litigators. They engage in trial preparation, interviewing parties and witnesses, finding experts, preparing exhibits, and writing briefs. Insurance defense attorneys usually try to get cases dismissed without going to trial. If they fail, they will often try to settle a case. Occasionally an insurance defense attorney does end up in court, where he or she will try to persuade the judge or jury that the client should not be liable for the injuries the plaintiff claims.

Intellectual Property

Intellectual property includes copyrights, trademarks, trade names, and patents. Intellectual property lawyers handle matters involving the registration of trademarks, infringement, protection of software, use of the Internet, trade secrets, unfair competition, and the use of brand names and celebrity endorsements. Patent lawyers are particularly specialized; many of them also hold degrees in engineering.

International

The nations of the world must interact with one another as they go about their daily business, both on a governmental and a private level, so a body of international law has arisen to govern these interactions. International affairs are governed by official agreements between nations such as treaties and conventions, customary international law that arises out of accepted standard practices between nations, and sometimes general principles of national law. Most nations belong to at least one international organization; the United Nations is the best-known of these. All members of an international organization agree at least nominally to follow the same agreements, which can govern trade, dispute resolution, use of shared resources, travel, and other topics that are common to the group of nations.

Labor

Labor law, not to be confused with employment law, concentrates on the relationship between labor unions and employers. It includes membership in labor organizations, collective bargaining, and strikes. This area is regulated by the National Labor Relations Act and other federal and state statutes, some of which are specific to particular industries.

Litigation (Trial Work)

Litigation is the process of bringing a case to trial. Lawyers who regularly argue cases in court are often called litigators. They spend weeks, months, or years researching the facts of a case, preparing arguments, filing documents with the court, and arguing cases. Much of their time is spent in the process of discovery, in which they interview witnesses and examine documents in order to determine the facts of a case.

Malpractice

Medical malpractice attorneys handle cases in which plaintiffs accuse doctors of having made mistakes in medical treatment. They work with doctors, hospitals, and insurers. Determining whether a mistake has occurred involves knowing the "standard of care" for a given condition, i.e. the type of treatment that doctors generally agree is appropriate. Attorneys in this field often employ nurse consultants to help them prepare cases.

Mergers and Acquisitions

Mergers and acquisitions, or M & A, is a branch of corporate law that deals with companies purchasing and/or merging with other companies. It also covers companies breaking up into smaller companies. Mergers and acquisitions can be extremely complicated, involving billions of dollars and thousands of employees. Attorneys who specialize in this area help companies negotiate prices, decide what to do with the employees and executives of a company that will no longer exist, determine the distribution of corporate stock, and figure out the tax consequences. They also help companies seek approval from the Securities Exchange Commission and other regulatory bodies. Attorneys may also have to pick up the pieces if a merger or acquisition fails to happen. This work requires a good understanding of federal and state laws governing corporations and a great attention to detail.

Plaintiffs' Attorneys

Plaintiffs' attorneys specialize in bringing lawsuits on behalf of plaintiffs. They may sue for negligence, products liability, medical malpractice, toxic torts, or any number of other claims. Plaintiffs' attorneys must put together entire cases, gathering evidence, questioning witnesses, making presentations to illustrate to jurors how accidents occurred. They can spend a lot of time meeting with judges and in court. Most cases, however, settle before trial, and plaintiffs' attorneys try to negotiate the best settlements possible. Plaintiffs' attorneys usually take payment in the form of a contingency, i.e., they take a percentage of the money that the plaintiff wins. This means that a plaintiffs' attorney must do all the up-front work in a case without pay. Don't enter this field unless you have a high tolerance for uncertainty!

Products Liability

Products liability law covers the responsibility that a manufacturer has for any damage done by a product it produces. For example, if a baby crib is designed in such a way that babies catch their heads in the slats, the crib's manufacturer can be liable for any injuries caused by this defect. Most states have their own products liability laws. Plaintiffs' attorneys bring many products liability lawsuits on behalf of their clients. Some defense firms specialize in defending products liability lawsuits.

Real Estate/Property

Property is a large and complicated field covering the ownership and use of possessions, real property such as land and buildings on it, and personal property, which includes anything other than land and buildings. It is a very old field and still uses terminology that dates back to medieval England: fee simple, fee tail, freehold estates, and the dreaded rule against perpetuities. Anyone who buys or sells a house or other property needs a real estate attorney. They do title searches, investigate zoning requirements, and perform closings; some do residential transactions, some do commercial, and some do both.

Tax

Tax lawyers are a particularly specialized bunch; many of them have a special advanced law degree called an LL.M. (Master of Laws). The federal and state tax codes are immensely complicated and change every year; it takes a real expert to keep up with them.

Tax lawyers specialize in making sure their clients pay as little tax as legally possible.

Torts

Torts are injuries, including physical injuries, mental and emotional injuries, and damage to property. Anyone who is injured in an accident and sues over it is involved in a tort lawsuit. Torts include trespass, fraud, intentional infliction of emotional distress, battery, products liability, and others. Victims of torts hope to recover damages of money for pain and suffering, lost earnings or earning capacity, and medical expenses. Plaintiffs are usually represented by lawyers who specialize in bringing lawsuits, called plaintiffs' attorneys; many plaintiffs' attorneys specialize in personal injury cases. Anyone who is sued needs an attorney who can defend against a lawsuit, often found in a defense firm; many defense firms specialize in insurance defense work, defending lawsuits whose defense is being paid for by an insurance company.

Toxic Torts

A toxic tort is a personal injury lawsuit in which the plaintiff claims that he or she has been injured or made ill by exposure to a toxic chemical. Asbestos, lead paint, pesticides, Agent Orange, atomic radiation, and toxic landfills have all formed the basis of toxic tort lawsuits. Attorneys who bring toxic tort lawsuits may suggest that the defendant has been negligent in allowing people to be exposed to the hazardous substance, or that it has used a product in a way that is unreasonably dangerous. Winning a toxic tort claim usually requires expert witnesses who can testify as to the risks involved with the substance in question. Some law firms specialize in bringing toxic tort claims to court. Because toxic tort claims are also often class actions, bringing one to court involves a huge expenditure of time, money, and manpower, but the payoffs can be huge.

Transactional Work

Some attorneys rarely or never go to court or handle cases that involve litigation. These attorneys are called transactional lawyers. Their work is done mostly in an office and may include writing contracts, drafting wills, creating trusts, negotiating with clients, and filing applications with government agencies. Attorneys who specialize in tax, trusts and estates, patents and trademarks, and corporate law are often transactional attorneys.

Trusts and Estates

Trusts and estates, or estate planning, is the field of law concerned with distributing property after death. No one has to write a will; every state has rules of descent and distribution that determine who gets what if someone dies intestate. But people with a lot of money and property, or those with complicated family situations, often want a more specific solution-they want particular people to get particular things, they want to create trusts to provide for their children, they want their descendants to avoid heavy tax burdens-and that is where estate planning can be very valuable.

White Collar Crime

White collar crime is a non-violent crime such as embezzlement, price fixing, fraud, perjury, securities fraud, or extortion. Computer fraud, mail fraud, and identity theft are white collar crimes that are increasing. These crimes are traditionally committed by fairly well-to-do individuals who work in offices in suits, hence the name "white collar." White collar crimes may involve large amounts of money and complicated trails of documents. It can include some types of organized crime. This type of case is different from the stereotypical criminal case, such as theft or murder, because the evidence may be entirely electronic and the harm difficult to identify. Federal and state prosecutors' offices now have departments that specialize in the prosecution of white collar crime. Some criminal defense lawyers specialize in defending these cases.

Workers' Compensation

Workers' compensation requires employers to compensate employees who are injured, made ill, or killed while at work. Injured employees do not have to prove that their employer was at fault or that they were not; they collect compensation regardless. In return, they give up the right to sue their employers for causing their injuries. Lawyers who specialize in workers' compensation may represent either injured employees who believe that they have not been adequately

Problem Solving

Becoming a Law Professor

Do you think you might like to teach in law school? You could aim to become a law professor, a profession with a high level of job satisfaction and somewhat more flexibility than legal practice. Law professors teach classes on specific legal topics, such as contracts, torts, or intellectual property; usually professors teach subjects that are related to their practice experience and their fields of research. In addition to teaching, law professors write articles for law reviews and may serve as consultants to businesses or law firms. So how does one become a law professor? Go to a highly ranked law school, get extremely good grades, serve on law review, earn a prestigious judicial clerkship, and practice for a few years with an illustrious law firm. Then write some learned articles on advanced legal topics, publish them in law reviews, and start applying for jobs. Easy!

compensated or employers who do not want to pay workers' compensation claims.

Private Practice

The two main types of private practice employers are law firms and corporations. The majority of lawyers in the United States work in private practice, most of them in law firms. A law firm is a business that exists to provide legal services to clients. It can employ any number of attorneys, plus related support staff such as paralegals and secretaries. Although the majority of law firms in the United States are small, with one to 20 attorneys working in them, there are a number of very large firms with more than 1,000 attorneys. A law firm that consists of only one lawyer is called a solo practice. Law firms come in a variety of structures:

• **Sole Proprietorship.** In this arrangement, one lawyer owns the firm and is responsible for everything: finding clients, performing work, collecting payment. If a client wants to sue the firm, the sole lawyer is the only one to sue.

- **Partnership.** In the old days, most firms were true partnerships; many still are today. That means that the partners own the firm and govern it together. They share the costs and profits in whatever percentages they decide on.

- **Limited Liability Partnership (LLP).** Because general partnerships are so risky, many law firms have chosen to become LLPs. In this arrangement, the owners are still partners but they are not individually liable for the negligence of their partners.

- **Limited Liability Company (LLC).** An LLC is similar to an LLP. The lawyer-owners are called "members" instead of partners. The owners have only limited liability for the firm's actions or debts. A solo practitioner may form an LLC as a way of protecting himself or herself from lawsuits.

- **Corporation.** A law corporation performs legal work for clients. The attorney-owners own shares of stock in the corporation. Although these attorneys might still be called partners, some firms have gone so far as to rename them "shareholders." The partners are not individually liable for the law firm's actions or debts. In exchange for this personal protection, the corporation may pay more in taxes than a partnership would. Only lawyers can own stock in a professional corporation devoted to legal work.

- **Professional Association (PA).** This arrangement is basically the same as a corporation or LLC.

The two main types of attorneys who work at law firms are partners, or owners, and associates, or employees who are on track to become partners. Firms also hire contract attorneys to do temporary jobs, or staff attorneys who are employees of the firm but not on track for partnership. The attorneys of a law firm may take on specific jobs within the firm, such as hiring or management. Many large corporations employ their own lawyers to handle legal matters for the company. Corporate attorneys are often called "in-house counsel." Their work can include writing letters, drafting and reviewing contracts, and watching to make sure the company commits no crimes.

Many law firms organize their lawyers into practice groups, each concentrating on a particular specialty. For example, one group of lawyers may do all of the firm's employment law work. Another group may focus on real estate, while another handles construction. One partner leads (or several partners lead) each group, communicating with clients and assigning work to the associates and paralegals who belong to the group. When an associate or paralegal enters a firm, he or she is assigned to a particular practice group and works mostly with that group.

Arbitrator or Mediator

Arbitrators and mediators specialize in helping parties solve disputes without going to trial. A mediator is a neutral third party who tries to help the parties solve their problems on their own. An arbitrator is a neutral third party who listens to both sides of the dispute and then decides which side should prevail. Many arbitrators and mediators practice law in law firms and do alternative dispute resolution as part of their practice.

Associate

Associates are lawyers who are employees of a law firm. The partners hire them and pay them a salary. When law students and recent graduates apply for jobs at law firms, they are usually hired as associates.

Associates typically work with a partner or team of partners and associates in a particular practice area. They begin by working on simple matters and doing legal research, and gradually work their way up to having more responsibility and contact with clients. Many associates hope to eventually "make partner," or to be invited to become a partner at the law firm. Although every firm has its own policies, this typically takes seven full-time years. Associates who take time off for some reason, such as women who take maternity leave, often take longer than seven years to make partner.

Contract Attorney

Contract attorneys are lawyers who do legal jobs on a contract, or temporary, basis. They are usually independent contractors rather than employees of a firm or corporation. That means they are paid by the hour or by the job instead of a salary, and the firm they work for provides them no benefits such as health insurance or a retirement plan. Many contract attorneys find work through legal employment agencies. Others form ad hoc relationships with law firms or other employers. Firms often hire contract attorneys to perform time-consuming high-volume tasks such as large-scale document reviews. Many young law school graduates find themselves working as contractors because they cannot find full-time jobs and look on this work as a way of building valuable experience that will lead to better jobs. Other attorneys choose to work as contract attorneys because they do not want to commit their entire lives to working at a conventional legal job. Contractors have some flexibility in picking and choosing their jobs, which can allow for more time off and greater freedom.

General Counsel (Chief Legal Officer)

A general counsel is the head lawyer in a corporate or government legal department. Also called the chief legal officer, or CLO, the general counsel must lead the legal department, ensure that the corporation's actions are all legal, and communicate regularly with the corporation's other officers. He or she also may handle the hiring of external counsel for matters that require more legal support than can be provided in-house. Corporations especially value general counsels who have good business judgment and who can explain legal issues in business terms. General counsels can make a very good living; in 2007, the highest-paid CLOs in the Southeast earned close to a million dollars a year, with bonuses and corporate stock awards making up most of that amount.

Hiring Partner

The hiring partner of a firm handles hiring new attorneys. The hiring partner may head a recruiting committee that solicits and examines résumés from law students and other prospective new hires, conducts on-campus interviews, and decides which students will be called in for second interviews (callbacks) and decides which will be offered jobs in summer associate programs. At the end of the summer program, the hiring partner will make offers of permanent employment to some of those students. In smaller firms, a hiring partner may work on his or her own, without a committee.

In-House Counsel

In-house counsel are attorneys who work for corporations, usually in corporate legal departments. They are called "in-house counsel" because they work for the corporation rather than for an outside organization such as a law firm. In-house attorneys perform many of the same tasks as attorneys in private practice at firms: research, writing briefs, drafting contracts, and negotiating deals on behalf of the company. They may provide advice to human resources on employment law matters, such as hiring, firing, pay, or discrimination. They handle matters such as intellectual property, mergers and acquisitions, or lawsuits against the corporation.

Managing Partner

A managing partner is a lawyer who manages an entire law firm. He or she may take on this role after years of practice as a lawyer. Managing a firm requires a different set of skills from practicing law. Managing partners must coordinate practice groups, watch over the firm's finances, work with human resources to keep the firm fully staffed and the employees happy, and make plans for the firm's future. Managing partners must have good leadership and communication skills and the ability to see the big picture of the firm's activities. A managing partner needs to understand financial matters, ethics, and the basic principles of running a business. A managing partner often limits his or her actual practice of law because running a firm can be a full-time job in itself.

Non-Equity Partner

In a law firm with a two-tier partnership arrangement, the lower tier of partners do not share ownership of the firm. These partners, called non-equity partners, are listed on the firm's masthead as partners and they do partner-level work, but they are still employees who receive a salary instead of a share of the profits. The big difference between non-equity partners and associates is that non-equity partners have employment contracts with the firm, whereas associates typically do not and can be fired at any time for any reason. Attorneys may remain at the non-equity partner level for several years before being made full partners. Some attorneys choose never to become full partners, preferring the non-equity arrangement.

Of Counsel

Some attorneys work with a law firm but in a capacity other than that of partner or associate. Of counsel attorneys may work part-time or on an as-needed basis. Usually there is no expectation that an of counsel attorney will eventually become a partner, though occasionally a firm will bring in a new experienced attorney and put him or her on of counsel status during a probationary period before making him or her a partner. Sometimes a partner will retire but remain at the firm of counsel, offering his or her expertise when needed. Some attorneys choose not to become partners, preferring the easier hours that often come with of counsel status.

Partner

Partners are lawyers who are the owners of a law firm. Partners are generally experienced attorneys who have practiced for several years and who have established relationships with clients. Partners do not receive a salary. Instead, they share the profits of the law firm's business after paying the firm's expenses, including salaries to associate attorneys. This means that while partners have the potential to make much more money than their employees, they also stand the chance of taking home no money during periods in which the firm is not bringing in a high income. If the law firm fails for some reason, the partners can lose everything. Partners also pay for their own benefits.

There are many different kinds of partnership arrangement. In some law firms, all partners share equally in profits and expenses. In others, some partners receive a greater share of profits than others. Some firms call their partners "shareholders," which reflects the fact that many law firms are not in fact true partnerships but instead limited liability companies, corporations, or other structures.

Summer Associate

Summer associates are law students who spend their summers working at law firms, doing the sort of work that low-level associates would do. Law firms use summer associate programs to recruit future lawyers. If a law firm likes a summer associate's work, it may offer him or her a job upon graduation from law school. Summer associate programs often present the law firm in the best possible light; summer associates are taken to dinners and parties and given interesting work in the hope that they will like the firm. Salaries can be quite good; many firms pay summer associates a weekly rate based on what they pay current first-year associates. Being a summer associate can be great fun. Being a real associate can also be fun but will almost certainly be much more work than being a summer associate. Don't assume your real job will be just like your summer experience!

Staff Attorney

A staff attorney works as an employee of a firm, company, or court but is not an associate and is not on a partnership track. Some attorneys who work at law firms have no wish to become partners, preferring the more stable hours and steady salary of a staff attorney. Sometimes a firm will decide that it does not want an associate to become a partner, but wants him or her to keep working as a staff attorney or permanent associate.

Solo Practitioner

Many lawyers work alone, running a legal practice without any other lawyers. Any lawyer who passes the state bar can hang out a shingle. Solo practitioners face all the challenges of running a business on their own. They must find their own clients and handle all business arrangements, such as renting office space, purchasing office supplies and furniture, and hiring and firing support staff. Some solo practitioners hire a legal secretary and a paralegal to help them. Solo practice has some advantages: the lawyer can choose how he or she wants to work, and does not have to share profits with anyone. It also has disadvantages: the single lawyer is responsible for finding and completing all the firm's work, however long it may take.

Public Sector Practice

Some attorneys work for the government as opposed to private clients. States, local governments, and the federal government all employ a number of attorneys. The Internal Revenue Service, U.S. Citizenship and Immigration Services, and other agencies need many lawyers to handle their daily work. Attorneys in public law may do all the same jobs as attorneys in private practice, such as handling litigation, dealing with real estate or employment or tax issues, and working on bond issues or other matters. Criminal prosecutions are all done in the public sector. Most judges are former attorneys who now serve in the government. Attorneys who work in the public sector tend to make much less money than their colleagues in private practice, but many find that public sector jobs give them the opportunity to do much more interesting work sooner than they would at a law firm. The public sector is also a common path to political office.

Attorney General

The attorney general is a government's main lawyer. The U.S. attorney general is the head of the U.S. Department of Justice and a member of the president's cabinet. The President nominates the attorney general, who must then be confirmed by the Senate. Each state has its own attorney general, who advises the government on legal matters. Most state attorneys general are elected.

City Attorneys and State Attorneys

Cities and states hire attorneys to represent them in legal matters. These attorneys review contracts, negotiate deals, examine the legality of the city's or state's policies, and handle any lawsuits that are brought against the city or state.

Head Counsel/Chief Counsel/Division Counsel

Governmental agencies such as the Internal Revenue Service employ a number of lawyers to handle litigation, draft documents and regulations, and write advisory opinions. The head counsel or chief counsel is the attorney in charge of the agency. A deputy head counsel might run a department within an agency. A division counsel is the attorney in charge of a division. These attorneys direct the work of staff attorneys and paralegals.

Judge

A judge runs a court of law. Judges preside over trials, listening to testimony from both sides of a case and running the proceedings. In a bench trial, the judge or judges decide the outcome of the case. In a jury trial, the judge runs the proceedings but the jury decides the outcome. When they are not sitting in court, judges review pleadings and briefs that argue the different sides of lawsuits, meet with attorneys to set schedules, and write opinions explaining their reasoning in cases. The opinions of judges become part of the body of common law and serve as guidelines for attorneys and judges in future cases. There are many levels of judges, from magistrate judges who preside over small courts (often found in strip malls) to the justices of the state and federal supreme courts. Every state has its own conventions for selecting judges; some judges are appointed, while others are elected. Many judges spend part of their career as trial lawyers before moving to the bench.

Law Clerk (Judicial Clerk)

Law clerks are law school graduates who work for judges doing research on legal issues and writing judicial opinions. A clerkship usually lasts for one year. Many law students want to become law clerks so that they can gain experience, get to know a judge, and to make themselves more marketable to employers. The competition for judicial clerkships is fierce, and typically the students with the best grades from the highest ranked schools get the really good ones. Students apply for clerkships in the fall of their final year in law school. The most prestigious clerkships are those with the U.S. Supreme Court, the state supreme courts, the 13 federal appeals courts, and some federal district courts. Many law clerks go on to jobs with law firms. A few clerks end up working for their judges permanently. Some law clerks later become law professors or judges themselves; about half of the justices on the U.S. Supreme Court were themselves clerks for the Supreme Court back at the beginnings of their careers.

Legal Aid Attorney

Many cities and counties have legal aid programs designed to assist low-income individuals with their civil legal concerns. Attorneys who work in legal aid programs may help people with workers' compensation problems, divorce and child custody issues, real estate, bankruptcy, and anything else that comes their way. Some legal services organizations specialize in issues such as immigration.

Legal services attorneys can be very busy, with a great deal of client contact and many court appearances. Language skills are often an asset for attorneys in this field. Legal aid attorneys generally earn less than they could in the private sector but may have greater job satisfaction.

Prosecutors and District Attorneys

Prosecutors are attorneys who prosecute people who are accused of crimes. They meet regularly with law enforcement officers and judges to decide how to handle the accused. They gather evidence, argue cases in court, enter into plea bargains, and propose sentences. Most counties have their own prosecutors. Different states call their prosecutors by different names. Many states call them district attorneys, or D.A.s. Others call them prosecutors. In South Carolina, county solicitors are in charge of prosecuting alleged criminals. Some states have a district attorney who oversees criminal prosecutions throughout the state. Depending on the state, head prosecutors or district attorneys may be elected or appointed by an elected executive, such as a governor. These attorneys then hire lower-level attorneys, paralegals, and other staff.

Fast Facts

How Does a Court Reporter Take Down Every Word Spoken in a Trial or Deposition?

Although a few court reporters still use shorthand (a hand-written code that allows a person to write very quickly), most today use either stenotype machines or stenomasks, supplemented with tape recorders. A stenomask looks a little like an oxygen mask. The court reporter holds it over his or her face and whispers into it every word spoken during the proceeding. The machine records everything he or she says and creates a transcript using voice-recognition software. Stenomasks can produce extremely accurate transcripts, and they are much easier to learn to use than shorthand or stenotype, which can take several years to master.

Public Defender

Public defenders defend people accused of crimes. Many accused individuals are too poor to hire attorneys themselves. Because every American citizen is guaranteed a defense attorney if accused of a crime, states, counties, and cities have developed various ways of providing public defenders. Some states have public defenders offices and pay attorneys to work full-time for poor defendants. In some cases, public defenders and prosecutors receive about the same salary, which is almost always less than the attorneys working there could receive in the private sector. Attorneys in the federal public defenders' office are paid fairly well. Some states do not employ public defenders, and instead assign indigent defense cases to the attorneys who belong to the state bar on a pro-bono basis.

Solicitor General

The solicitor general is the U.S. government's own lawyer. He or she argues cases for the president before the U.S. Supreme Court. The solicitor general traditionally wears a morning suit with a long tailcoat when appearing before the Supreme Court.

Staff Attorney

Just like law firms, governmental agencies hire attorneys to handle day-to-day business such as legal research and writing, litigation, negotiations, and other legal transactions. Staff attorneys are employees who receive a salary. Though there is no partnership track within governmental practice, staff attorneys can move up to positions of authority such as division counsel or chief counsel. Staff attorneys make up for their relatively lower salary with saner hours than those of law firm attorneys, more job security, and potential government pension plans.

United States Attorneys

U.S. attorneys represent the U.S. federal government in federal district and appeals courts in both criminal and civil cases. They are part of the U.S. Department of Justice. The President appoints U.S. attorneys to terms of four years. There are 93 U.S. attorneys spread throughout the states and U.S. territories. U.S. attorneys are assisted in their work by assistant attorneys and other staff members.

Legal Staff and Support Jobs

Law firms and other legal employers need many employees who are not lawyers. Legal secretaries and paralegals are essential to the efficient practice of law. Specialists in finance, human resources, technology, and other areas can also find many jobs in the legal field.

Chief Financial Officer

Some law firms are large enough to employ a chief financial officer to handle budgeting, financial planning, forecasting, profitability analysis, accounting, tax planning and reporting, payroll, pension plans, and other financial management. Billing and collections may be a major part of this job. Compiling billable hours or other bases for billing, sending out bills, and pursuing payment can take up a great deal of time. Individuals in this role generally have a financial background or an MBA.

Client Services Coordinator

A client services coordinator maintains a law firm's relationships with its clients. This can include communicating with clients about the status of their cases, scheduling meetings, making travel arrangements, planning parties, sending presents, and doing anything else necessary to keep up good client relationships. Most law firms will want someone with at least a bachelor's degree for this job.

Courier

Law firms employ couriers to deliver documents quickly. A courier's most important job is to get pleadings and other legal documents delivered to the courthouse and the correct parties on time. It is not unusual for an attorney to work on a brief or pleading until nearly the last possible moment on the day it is due; the courier must then race it to the courthouse before the end of the working day. Couriers may also deliver documents to attorneys within the same law firm.

Court Reporter

A court reporter, or stenographer, sits in court hearings, depositions, or other proceedings in which people testify under oath and transcribes the exact words of that testimony. After a hearing or deposition, the court reporter creates an official transcript of the event, in which everything that was said is reproduced verbatim. The National Court Reporters Association certifies members; a court reporter must be able to reproduce at least 225 words per minute. Prospective court reporters can get their training at business colleges, colleges, universities, or online. Court reporters can make a good income. The median salary for full-time court reporters is $42,000, but many court reporters make over $100,000. If you want to work as a freelancer, this is a great area for you. Fewer people have been entering the field in recent years, but the need for reporters has been growing, so there will be ample opportunity to work.

Director of Human Resources

Most large companies and law firms have a director of human resources who may or may not be a lawyer. The director of human resources handles matters related to employees in the firm or corporation. He or she identifies positions that need to be filled, advertises jobs, interviews prospective candidates, and hires new employees. The director of human resources also handles training, performance evaluation, salaries, benefits such as health insurance and retirement plans, workers' compensation, discipline, and the termination or layoff of employees.

Electronic Discovery Specialist

Do you like working with computers? Electronic discovery, or e-discovery, is a growing field, and there is great demand for paralegals who can do it. E-discovery professionals specialize in discovery involving electronically stored information, or ESI. In electronic discovery, attorneys are looking for essentially the same materials they would want from paper discovery, but all the information is contained in electronic documents such as e-mails and computer files. The area of e-discovery is quite new to the law, and many lawyers and paralegals are still somewhat uncomfortable working with ESI. E-discovery professionals start as information technology workers, paralegals, or even as attorneys. At the moment, most e-discovery specialists learn the field through hands-on experience or continuing legal education seminars. Workers skilled in this area can make good money, well over $100,000 a year in some markets.

Information Technology Manager

The information technology manager or systems manager of a law firm or legal practice handles computer and telecommunications issues, including selecting computers and applications, installing and updating systems, and setting up data storage and records management. The IT manager may be in charge of choosing legal research systems. There are a number of litigation support and legal practice programs now available, and a good IT manager will ensure that these are fully implemented. The IT manager may train lawyers, paralegals, and secretaries in how to use their systems.

Law Firm Administrator

Law firms often employ office administrators or general managers to oversee operation of the business. This allows attorneys to dedicate their time to practicing law instead of handling management needs.

On the Cutting
Edge

Trial Technology Consultant

A trial technology consultant, or trial technologist, specializes in using technology in the courtroom. Computerized graphics, movies, computer-generated animation, and multimedia presentations can help an attorney convey the facts of a case to a jury more effectively. Trial technologists work with attorneys during trial preparation to create videos, charts, graphics, working models, and other technological exhibits. During a trial, the technology consultant will set up audiovisual equipment and run the videos and other displays when called upon. Trial technology consultants need training in audio and video editing, presentation software, and information technology. This field is expected to grow as more attorneys adopt high-tech trial techniques.

The head administrator may be called executive director, business manager, or chief operating officer. Depending on the size of the firm, the office administrator may handle financial planning, payroll, recruiting of staff and/or lawyers, facilities management, risk management, marketing, client development, and overseeing the legal practice. Office administrators may buy supplies, order repairs, maintain up-to-date computer systems, schedule and organize parties, and choose insurance policies. In larger firms, there may be several different managers who specialize in these various areas, but in smaller firms one administrator may handle everything.

Good administrators need to understand accounting and finance, human resources, the way the legal industry works, and the fundamentals of project management. There are no specific training programs for law firm administrators. A college degree is not absolutely necessary, though law firms may prefer to hire university graduates for this job. Many legal administrators are trained as certified public accountants. Others learn their skills by working as paralegals, serving in the military, or gaining other experience in business.

Law Librarian

If you like books and online research, you may like being a law librarian. Law librarians manage law firms' collections of legal materials and help lawyers with their research. This job has changed tremendously over the past two decades. In the 1980s almost all legal research was done in libraries, with printed volumes of court cases and statutes. Many law firms devoted an entire room to their collection of reference materials. Lawyers in small firms that could not afford to buy full libraries had to make trips to courthouse libraries to use the collections there. Today most legal research is done online. As a result, some law firms have gotten rid of their physical libraries. Law librarians are still in demand, however, both in law firms and at courthouses and law schools.

Modern law librarians now spend much of their time on non-legal research, marketing, and negotiating contracts with online research services and recovering the costs for those services from clients. Librarians today need to have expertise in electronic document storage and retrieval as well as in the law. Most law librarians come to the field with a graduate degree in library science; about 30 percent of law librarians have a JD. A JD is not a requirement for most positions (it is for most law school libraries), though a degree in library science is, so aspiring law librarians would do best to focus their studies on library science instead of going to law school.

Litigation Support Professional

A litigation support professional is a paralegal or legal assistant who specializes in large-scale litigation. Some lawsuits are enormous, involving millions of documents and thousands of people. Legal assistants have expertise in managing this high volume of data. The key difference between an ordinary paralegal and a litigation support professional is that the litigation support professional is skilled in the use of technology. Many have an information technology background, which helps them with the technological side of litigation prep, such as using case management software and document management programs, and participating in electronic discovery. Litigation support professionals are in high demand, and demand is expected to increase.

Legal Consultant

Legal consultants help lawyers organize their businesses. Often former lawyers with legal practice experience, legal consultants offer help in organizing firms, hiring administrators, developing strategies for handling large projects, maintaining client relationships, and improving workplace morale and work-life balance. They may also help firms develop strategies for adapting the business to a changing world. Consultants with legal training understand the challenges of the profession and confidentiality requirements.

Legal Document Assistant

A legal document assistant is not a lawyer but specializes in the preparation of legal documents. This position is common in California, where a 1998 law created a formal profession known as legal document assistant, or LDA. Unlike paralegals, LDAs in California can provide legal document services directly to clients, without the supervision of a lawyer. They are often used by clients who want to represent themselves in court. LDAs do not provide legal advice to their clients, nor can they appear in court on a client's behalf.

Legal Nurse Consultant/Nurse Paralegal

Legal nurse consultants (LNCs) are nurses who specialize in helping lawyers understand medical information. LNCs work for lawyers who handle cases in the fields of personal injury, wrongful death, workers' compensation, medical malpractice, products liability, and other areas that involve physical injuries or illnesses. They read and analyze medical records, interpret doctors' notes, find medical experts, interview plaintiffs and medical experts, do medical research, and arrange medical examinations. They may prepare reports, charts, or timelines that illustrate a patients' medical history in a way that is easy for a jury to understand. LNCs may also testify as expert witnesses at trials or depositions. LNCs are registered nurses with several years nursing experience who have obtained an additional certification as legal nurse consultants. Some work full-time as employees of law firms. Others work as independent contractors for an hourly rate. Hourly pay for LNCs can be as high as $200.

Legal Secretary

Are you really good at paying attention to details? Then you might like working as a legal secretary. A legal secretary works for an attorney often answering the telephone and placing phone calls. He or she may prepare letters and legal documents as directed by attorneys. Secretaries may be responsible for assembling the correct papers for mailings or filings, including making the correct number of copies and collecting the proper signatures. (Does that sound easy? It is not; some legal documents need to reach a large number of people, and it is the secretary's job to make sure everyone who is supposed to receive or sign a document does.) A legal secretary may be responsible for locating or organizing documents related to a case. Some legal secretaries also serve as office managers.

Paralegal (Legal Assistant)

Paralegals (sometimes called legal assistants) do all sorts of legal jobs. In many cases, paralegals do the same work that lawyers do, but entirely under the supervision of a lawyer. Paralegals perform legal research, write legal memos and letters, interview witnesses, conduct title searches, deliver documents to courthouses, and handle many other tasks. They often manage time-consuming tasks such as organizing documents and preparing exhibits for trial. Paralegals cannot appear in court, set fees for legal services, sign legal documents and pleadings on behalf of a party to a case, give legal advice, or establish an attorney-client relationship. Those restrictions prevent paralegals from offering legal services on their own.

Receptionist

Large firms need a person to greet people who call or walk in. A receptionist must answer the telephone, transfer calls to the correct recipients, take messages, greet clients and other individuals who walk in the front door, send them to the correct office or meeting room, and otherwise ensure that visitors and callers are smoothly connected with the right attorneys. Though the job may seem simple, it is actually quite difficult to present a good first impression all the time. Good receptionists, with excellent people skills, diplomacy, and patience, are highly sought after.

Recruiting Coordinator

Many medium-sized and large law firms employ a non-lawyer, to coordinate recruiting of new employees. Any résumés sent to the firm will end up on the desk of the recruiting coordinator, who will read them and choose the ones that look the best. The recruiting coordinator may then forward the strongest résumés to the hiring partner or recruiting committee, who will proceed with the interview process. The recruiting coordinator may conduct interviews of paralegals, secretaries, and other staff.

Trial Consultant (Jury Consultant)

Trial consultants work with attorneys to help them argue cases more effectively. Attorneys realize that presenting a case in court involves more than just knowing the law. To persuade a jury, an attorney must craft the strongest possible argument, and then present it with attention to every detail. Trial consultants participate at all phases of a trial, starting with discovery and proceeding through the preparation of exhibits and arguments, the selection of witnesses and experts, and the choice of jurors. They help lawyers decide which arguments are the strongest, and may help them compose their opening and closing statements.

Trial consulting firms may set up mock trials with fake judges and jurors to allow attorneys and parties to make a practice run of a trial; the consultants then analyze the reactions of the mock participants to see what works and what could be improved. Some trial consultants specialize in psychology. Others are experts at graphic design, writing, or even theatre. Some are lawyers, but a law degree is not a requirement for this field. What is crucial is that the consultant understand human behavior and have good intuition.

Chapter 4

Tips for Success

The most important tip for success in the legal field is to pay attention to detail. Truth, justice, and millions of dollars can ride on small nuances of language, thought, and action. If you never take any detail for granted, you are less likely to make the sorts of careless mistakes that can have severe repercussions. From this key piece of advice follows a few, more specific tips.

First, mind your grammar. Law is a profession of language. Minor grammatical mistakes can substantially change the meaning of a sentence, which can have very big repercussions. Bad grammar also looks unprofessional. This applies even to e-mail; you may think your e-mail grammar does not matter, but there are many readers who think otherwise and will look down on you if you do not bother with capitals or punctuation. Second, always be polite. Although it should go without saying that you will always be polite to clients, it is just as important to be polite to those who work with you. Being courteous to superiors can get you better assignments, while being courteous to those who work for you will get you better results. If someone does you a favor, thank him or her! A workplace where people are polite to one another makes for a much nicer, more productive atmosphere. Third, get your work done on time. Does that seem obvious? You would be amazed how many people have difficulty with punctuality. In the law, some deadlines are very real. Federal courts wait for no man. Even if a federal judge will not fine you for being late, other people are depending on your work to arrive on a certain day, and perhaps even a certain hour.

Attention to detail, care with language, politeness and punctuality should begin well before one lands a job with a law firm. From the onset of your job search you should display these qualities. For instance, always find out the name of the person to whom you should address your résumé and transcript. This is easy to do. Check the firm's Web site, or call or e-mail the firm and ask. You stand a much better chance of getting an interview if you send your materials to the right person. After you interview for a job, send notes to the people who took the time to talk to you thanking them for doing so. Not only will it make them like you better, it will also remind them of your existence.

Keeping
in Touch

Number One Tip: Networking

Networking, or making and using contacts with other people for job purposes, may be the single most important thing you can do to make your legal career successful.

Career counselors tell their clients that most jobs are never advertised at all. Most jobs get filled by networking, or word-of-mouth. But networking is not just useful for finding jobs. A good network can facilitate nearly anything you try to do.

Do you need a job? Talk to friends and acquaintances who either work where you want to work or might know someone who does. Do you need help performing a task? Ask someone you think might know how; even if he or she cannot help you, you may find out who can. Do you want bankers to bring their work to your firm? Go to parties or events where you can meet them. Some networking can happen accidentally. Maybe you decide to take a sailing class, and who should share a boat with you but one of the bankers you wanted to meet! Now the two of you are friends, and maybe he will think of you if he needs legal work.

Anyone can form part of your network: family, friends, acquaintances, friends of friends. That is one good reason to always be polite; you never know when an acquaintance might be able to help you.

Becoming a Lawyer

Lawyer or Paralegal?

You may know for certain that you want to be a lawyer. Perhaps you have related experience in the field and would like to expand on that. Television, books, or personal experience may prod your thinking that litigation is for you. Maybe you want to fight for civil rights, end sexual harassment in the workplace, and handle corporate mergers while you are at it.

If you are like many prospective lawyers, however, you are considering law school mainly because it seems like a sure thing, a way to learn skills that will make you lots of money while earning you a certain social status. That is fine, and many excellent lawyers chose law school for those reasons. But if you are not sure why you want to go to law school, do think about it at least a little. Law school is expensive and prepares its graduates for one thing: practicing law. You may be a valuable worker in the legal field without it.

Warning: You may have heard that a law degree is a good preparation for any number of careers, not just the practice of law. While it is true that many law school graduates have established successful careers in various non-legal fields, getting a law degree is not necessarily the best way to embark on a non-legal career. The business world often values the MBA degree over the JD, and many non-legal employers are not sure exactly what skills a lawyer can offer them. Bottom line: if you are fairly certain you do not want to practice law, do not go to law school.

If you are unsure about your legal ambitions but think you would like to try working in the legal field, consider becoming a paralegal, at least temporarily. Paralegals make good money and can do nearly everything that lawyers do. You can become a paralegal in just a few months (or in no time at all) and for much less money than you would pay for law school. It is easier to find paralegal jobs than to find employment as an attorney. If, after working as a paralegal for a while, you do decide to go to law school and become an attorney, you will know what you are getting into!

Getting into Law School

If you want to become a lawyer, you almost certainly need to go to law school. Back in the old days, lots of people became attorneys simply by working for another lawyer for a few years and then taking the bar exam. Some jurisdictions still allow this; the California Bar, for example, allows people who worked in a law office or with a judge to take the bar exam. (The California bar exam is notoriously difficult.) If you are tempted to skip law school, check your state's requirements for bar admission. You might get away with it. For most people, though, law school is the only way to become a lawyer.

Your choice of law school will depend on a number of factors. These include location, cost, prestige, and your own interests.

Location. For many people, the first consideration in choosing a law school is its location. It may be most convenient to choose a law school close to where you now live. Or, if you know you want to practice somewhere else, it may be to your advantage to study law in that state. A third option is to use law school as an opportunity to experience living someplace new for a few years. You may also weigh such factors as climate, housing, availability of part-time jobs, and recreational opportunities.

Cost. Law school is expensive. Most law students leave school with large amounts of debt. Some law schools are more expensive than others, though. Prestigious private schools come with a high price tag. Tuition at Yale Law School for 2008-09 was $44,000. Public schools cost much less, especially for state residents. At Louisiana State University, for example, in 2008-09 residents of Louisiana paid $10,722; non-residents paid $19,818. Tuition increases are standard; most law schools increase their tuition every year.

Prestige. Ah, prestige. It is no secret that the highest-paying law firms recruit almost entirely from the top-ranked law schools. The annual listings in *U.S. News and World Report* actually do mean something in law firm recruiting. That does not mean that students from other schools cannot find jobs. It just takes them longer. (Typically almost all the graduates of a top-tier law school have jobs by graduation or shortly thereafter; at lower-ranked schools, large numbers of students will graduate still unemployed.) If you are serious about getting a prestigious judicial clerkship, landing a lucrative law firm job, or perhaps going into politics or teaching law a degree from a highly ranked law school can be an advantage.

Your Interests. Different law schools emphasize different aspects of law. Some have excellent programs in specialties such as environmental law or international law. Some have a large number of clinical programs to give students hands-on practice in legal skills. If you know what sort of practice you want to do, choosing a specialized program can help you.

There is one other factor that will almost certainly affect where you go to law school. That is admissions. Admission to top law schools is extremely competitive. Harvard Law School, for example, admits about 10 percent of applicants. Even less competitive schools deny admission to some applicants.

Most law schools look at two numbers when selecting applicants: GPA and LSAT score. Some schools even use a formula to compute an applicant's value based on those two numbers, and admit only those applicants who receive a certain score. Law schools also consider other factors, though, such as work experience, unique talents, and various types of diversity. Despite the popularity of LSAT prep courses, it is entirely possible to study for the LSAT on your own and do very well at it. If you have the time and money to spend on LSAT prep, and you think a class will help you apply yourself, by all means take one, but it is not obligatory.

Going to Law School

Law school generally lasts three academic years, or six full-time semesters. First-year students are called 1Ls. Second-year students are 2Ls, and third-years are 3Ls. Graduates of law school receive a degree called a JD, which stands for "juris doctor."

In law school, each class focuses on a specific area of the law. Most law schools require first-year students to take basic subjects such as contracts, torts, criminal law, civil procedure, property, and constitutional law. After that, students can choose their classes. They may take trusts and estates, international law, environmental law, evidence, trial advocacy, corporations, secured transactions, tax, and any number of other classes based on their interests and intended practice areas.

Many law professors teach using the Socratic method. This pedagogic technique, named after the teaching method used by the Greek philosopher Socrates, involves the professor calling on students in class and asking them to explain the points of the case du jour. This can be a very nerve-wracking experience, especially in a large class. Professors choose their victims in various ways. Some call on students at random, some go alphabetically through the class roll, and some actually prefer to use volunteers. To avoid embarrassment, learn your professor's methods, and try to be prepared!

Grades

Law school grades are important. Extremely important. Why? Employers look at grades to decide whom to hire; the higher a student's grades, the more likely he or she will get an offer from one of the highest-paying firms. The same goes for the most prestigious judicial clerkships.

First year grades are especially important. Why? Employers interview 2Ls for summer associate positions in the fall of their second year of law school. These summer positions often turn into offers of employment after graduation. The only grades employers can look at for these positions are the grades the students earned in their first year of law school. First-year grades are also the ones law reviews use to select their members. Good grades in the first two semesters can give students an advantage that can last for years.

So if grades are so important, how does a student get good ones? It would seem that getting good grades would be a simple matter of going to class, doing the assigned work, and studying before exams. This is not necessarily the case.

Some law schools grade on a curve, which means that the majority of the grades given in a class will be a particular letter—B, say, or B+. If the main grade is B, the grading system is said to be done on a "B mean." In such a class, between 60 and 80 percent of the grades will be some variety of B. That can leave as little as 10 percent of the grades for As, and another 10 percent for Cs. This type of grading is meant to remove the cut-throat pressure for grades that some schools have, and makes it virtually impossible to fail, but it also makes it very hard to stand out.

Percentages being what they are, only a few students in every law school class get the best grades. What about everyone else? It depends. At top-ranked law schools, almost every graduate can get a good job after graduation, though the students with worse grades may have to work harder to find work. (At these schools, all the students enter law school with very good credentials, such as excellent undergraduate grades and strong résumés, so they have other material to show prospective employers.) At other schools, weaker students may have a hard time finding work. Some law school graduates eventually give up on finding legal work and turn to other fields.

Law Review and Journals

Most law schools publish academic journals containing articles on legal topics written by scholars. The most prestigious of these journals are called "law reviews." Schools also publish specialty journals that focus on specific areas of law, such as environmental law, corporate law, or international law.

Law reviews and other law journals are unusual in academia in that they are edited entirely by students. Every year law students compete to be chosen for the staffs of these journals. Law review staffers usually come from the students who earned the best grades in their first semester or two; they are said to "grade on" to the law review. Other journals hold writing competitions, in which students write essays or edit articles as they would do as part of the editorial staff. Law reviews may select some of their staffers this way, too.

The staff of a law review or journal spends its time selecting articles for publication from those submitted by professional writers (law professors plus a few judges and lawyers who find the time to write articles) and editing them to ensure that their citations are correct. Law review and journal staffers are also expected to write their own publishable articles, called "notes," which may or may not be published. 2Ls serve as staffers, while 3Ls hold editorial positions.

Law review experience can be a big advantage in finding a job. Many judges and employers believe that working on the law review teaches valuable legal research and writing skills. Law professors, judges, and high-powered law firm partners are very often former law review staffers or editors.

Other Ways to Make Yourself Stand Out

Moot court is a type of mock trial competition in which students practice their skills at writing appellate briefs and performing oral arguments. It is extracurricular, so the students who participate must find time for this activity in addition to their classes. Participants work in teams of two. They study the facts of their cases, write appellate briefs, and argue their legal points before faux appellate judges.

The judges choose winners, who may then progress to regional or national tournaments. Separate awards are given for the best briefs. Law students who win moot court or brief competitions at any level are highly desirable to law firms.

Law schools sponsor a number of other competitions, including contests for best memo and best brief in first-year legal writing classes. Students may submit essays and articles to various writing contests. Client counseling, negotiation, and trial advocacy all generate competitions. Some competitions give monetary prizes to the winners; others just come with glory. All of them look good on a résumé.

Law professors must publish articles to keep up their professional credentials, but they have very little time to do the time-consuming research necessary to write these articles. That is where research assistants come in. Many law professors employ law students to work part time doing research on specialized topics and to organize the materials in a useful way. The pay is usually low, but the work can be interesting and the experience is valuable.

Clinics provide hands-on practice to students who want to do real legal work while still in law school. In clinics, students provide legal advice, do research, and draft documents for low-income people. Some states even allow students to try cases. Clinics specialize in areas such as domestic violence, immigration, labor, and gay and lesbian rights. Students who participate in clinics often receive valuable real-world experience.

The Order of the Coif is a legal honor society for those who graduate in the top ten percent of their law school classes. The society is roughly equivalent to Phi Beta Kappa at the undergraduate level. Students are notified after final law school grades are tabulated and class rank is calculated, which may be after graduation. Members receive a certificate, a badge, a key, and sometimes a coif (a close-fitting cap popular in medieval Europe). Membership in the Order of the Coif looks very good to future employers.

Entering the Bar

Graduation from law school is not the end of a law student's studies. Any graduate who wants to practice law must pass the bar exam of the state in which he or she wishes to work. A bar exam tests a lawyer's understanding of important areas of the law. Every state creates its own bar exam. Most of them take two or three full days.

Most new JDs spend much of the summer after graduation studying for the bar exam. Some students actually attend several weeks of class, known as "bar review." Bar review classes are offered by several companies that charge a premium price for exam preparation. It is also possible to buy law review materials and study at home.

The bar exam is typically offered twice a year, in late July and late February. A person who wants to take it must register with the state bar well ahead of the deadline, and usually must pay a hefty application fee. Bars often require recommendations and background checks as well.

Some jurisdictions require applicants to take the Multistate Bar Examination (MBE, popularly known as "the Multistate"), a six-hour, two-hundred-question multiple choice examination that covers contracts, constitutional law, criminal law, evidence, real property, and torts. Every state decides what score test takers must receive on the Multistate in order to be admitted to the bar.

Everyone
Knows

Almost all states also require lawyers to achieve a certain score on the Multistate Professional Responsibility Examination (MPRE), which tests a lawyer's understanding of ethics rules. This test is offered three times a year, but not at the same time as the bar exam. For more information on the MBE and MPRE, see (http://www.ncbex.org).

State bar exams may also include essay exams on various legal topics, such as trusts and estates, insurance, commercial paper, corporations, and tax. These questions are written and graded by members of the local bar.

Bar exams vary greatly in difficulty and pass rates. Some state bar exams are notoriously difficult and have a low pass rate. In California, for example, only 36.8 percent of those who took the February 2007 General Bar Exam passed. In North and South Dakota, on the other hand, bar passage rates over 90 percent are not uncommon.

Becoming a Law Staffer

Becoming a staff worker for a legal employer is much easier and faster than becoming an attorney. There are no hard and fast rules about how to get this type of job; legal secretaries, paralegals, and other staff workers are judged more on their ability to do the job than their educational background.

In the United States there are no formal requirements for becoming a paralegal in most states (California is the exception, requiring paralegals to complete a course of study in legal work.) and there are no licensing requirements. Some paralegals get their jobs with only a high school diploma. About 1,000 community colleges and universities throughout the United States now offer paralegal courses that will certify graduates, which can be helpful in finding jobs. Some of these programs require applicants to hold a college degree, while others will take students who have a high school degree or some college. Training includes courses in legal research, basic areas of law, the use of computers, claims investigation and discovery, and other practical topics. The ABA has approved about 260 paralegal training programs. Employers do not typically require this type of certification, but it certainly does not hurt. In addition, many paralegal training programs help their students and graduates find jobs. Some programs offer internships through which students can get experience working at law firms, corporations, or government offices.

More important than training is a paralegal's or legal secretary's ability to do his or her job. Attorneys want staff people they can trust to do the job right. If you understand legal terminology, know how to do research, and can present your findings to an attorney in a clear and useful way, you will have no trouble keeping your job. Experience is highly prized. In fact, attorneys have been known to covet one another's paralegals and even occasionally to tempt paralegals away from other law firms!

Though paralegals are not held to the same continuing legal education requirements as attorneys, they are allowed to attend CLE. (California requires paralegals to attend CLE.) It is a good idea for a paralegal to stay abreast of developments in his or her practice area.

One way to get ahead as a paralegal is to specialize. If you know all about bankruptcy, real estate and title searches, products liability, divorce, or some other in-demand field of law, you may have an easier time finding jobs.

If you want to become a legal secretary, you will need at least a high school diploma or GED. Then you will need to become competent at secretarial skills, such as typing and word processing. Community colleges offer classes in this area. You will probably want to take classes specifically on being a legal secretary. Legal secretaries must know a lot of legal terminology and understand what legal documents should look like. Certification offered by NALS can help, though it is not strictly necessary. Attention to detail and good organization are the most important qualities in a legal secretary. The secretary is the one who puts dates on the attorney's calendar, records messages, schedules meetings and airplane tickets, and handles all the other crucial details of an attorney's working life. Attorneys want secretaries who can do these things without asking lots of questions or making mistakes.

Many legal secretaries find good jobs by beginning as temps. Employment agencies know of many opportunities at law firms. If you take a temporary job and you and the attorney you work for decide you are a good fit, you may just have found a permanent position with a salary.

Skilled legal secretaries are highly prized by their employers. If you are successful, you may find yourself promoted to office manager, in charge of keeping the entire office running smoothly. Many veteran legal secretaries, though, have no interest in moving into management. They find the satisfaction (and salary) of doing a good job for the same attorneys for many years to be enough.

Finding a Job

Interviewing at Law School

During the fall, law schools swarm with law students in suits, all heading for meetings with recruiters from law firms and other employers. Major law firms, judges, and government agencies all work with law school placement offices to set up interviews with promising students. The system is fairly simple. Placement offices keep student résumés on file. If a student is interested in an employer, he or she signs up for an interview on the day the employer visits campus. The placement office sends copies of interested students' grades and résumés to that employer. Some schools allow the employer to select students for interviews. Other schools instead allow students to rank their favorite law firms and use a lottery to determine who gets on-campus slots. Most of the people interviewing at law school are 2Ls. Few employers want 1Ls, and 3Ls often have their jobs lined up already.

Once on-campus interviews are done, employers invite their favorite candidates to visit their offices. These visits are called "call-backs." During a call-back, students talk to attorneys about the work they do, see the facilities, and get an idea of what it would be like to work in the office. Law firms often take their candidates out to nice lunches and dinners and try to show them generous hospitality. At this point employers decide which students they like best and offer them jobs. Offers usually come very quickly after call-backs; sometimes a law firm will even offer a student a job during a callback, though it is also common for a firm to telephone the student a day or two after the interview. Rejections usually come in the mail.

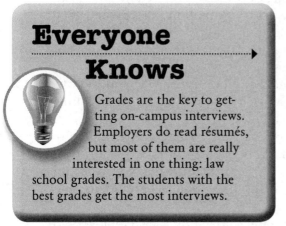

Everyone Knows

Grades are the key to getting on-campus interviews. Employers do read résumés, but most of them are really interested in one thing: law school grades. The students with the best grades get the most interviews.

Note that you do not have to wait for law firms to ask to interview you. Many law students have landed jobs by calling up firms in the city in which they plan to live, informing the firms that they will be in town on a certain day, and asking if they can come by to meet some of the attorneys. In many cases, the fact that you know you will be living in a certain town holds a lot of weight with employers.

Judicial Clerkships

If you are a really successful law student, chances are you'll be tempted to apply for a judicial clerkship. Judicial clerks spend a year or two after law school working for a judge. There are clerkships at all levels of the U.S. court system. The most prestigious clerkships are with the U.S. Supreme Court and the U.S. federal circuit courts of appeals.

Clerks spend their time assisting judges. Their work can include legal research, cite checking, drafting opinions for the judges, reading briefs from parties to lawsuits, and other clerical tasks. The median salary for clerks is not especially high, around $54,000 in 2008, but the experience is considered invaluable for an attorney's future career. Law firms and other employers will usually hold a space for a year if one of their recruits receives an offer for a judicial clerkship.

Generally law students apply for judicial clerkships in the fall of their third years. Law school placement offices help their students put together application packets, which include cover letters, résumés, writing samples, transcripts, and several letters of recommendation. Law students typically pay for their own travel to visit judges. Judges often offer clerkships during interviews, and it is customary for a student to accept or decline on the spot. Only apply for clerkships that you really want! Once a student has accepted a clerkship, he or she is bound to work for the judge that year; it is extremely bad form to back out of a clerkship once it has been accepted.

Acing Interviews

The most important thing to do before you show up at an interview is to prepare yourself. Find out about the employer. Know what sort of work the firm or agency does and what sort of work you would want to do there. Explain to yourself why you would be a good fit with that employer; if you do not know, your prospective employer certainly will not! The more you know about the employer, the more detailed your answers to interview questions will be. Never show up at an interview intending to "wing it"; your interviewers will be able to tell that you do not know what you are talking about.

Dress nicely. Dress as you imagine you would if you were going to work for that employer that day. Lawyers and law students should always interview in suits. If you are interviewing for a staff job, a suit is still a good idea, though you have a little more flexibility than lawyers. Women should avoid wearing too much makeup and neither men nor women should wear perfume.

The interview is your chance to sell yourself. Come up with a list of selling points. If you have got legal experience, think of your most significant legal achievements. If this is your first job, come up with other accomplishments that will show the employer your capabilities.

Here are some good questions to ask during an interview:

→ How is the firm organized? How many lawyers work in a particular department? Would I be assigned to a particular department or practice group?

➡ What responsibilities would I have?

➡ Who will assign me work? Will I have to request work?

➡ Will other departments ever assign me work?

➡ How many billable hours are expected? How do you calculate billable hours?

➡ How many years does it take to make partner?

➡ How are employees evaluated?

➡ What type of training do you give employees?

➡ What is the overall culture of the firm/organization? What do the interviewers like most about working there?

Be honest when answering questions. Do not exaggerate your accomplishments or skills. If you get hired on the basis of false information, you can get in big trouble.

Do not ask about salary, benefits, vacation, and other perks during your initial interview. If you get called back for more interviews, the employer will tell you all about the advantages of working there. At the interview, you simply want to prove that you are hardworking, intelligent, courteous, mature, and pleasant. This is your chance to make a positive first impression. Be enthusiastic! Make eye contact! The employer wants to know what you will be like around clients or in front of a judge. Those situations are stressful, much like interviews. If you can handle an interview with aplomb, that speaks well of your ability to handle other situations you may encounter at work.

Calibrate your interview manner to the person interviewing you. For example, imagine you are a law student interviewing for an associate position at a firm. If a group of young associates interviews you, they are much more concerned about your personality than about your ability to do legal work. They assume you are qualified, so you do not need to impress them with your grades or dedication. Instead, show them how likable you are; make them want to go out to lunch or out after work with you. A partner, on the other hand, is much more interested in your working ability. Talk about your favorite classes, your legal interests, and your drive to become an excellent attorney.

Never criticize your current employer. This looks disloyal, and gives the interviewer a bad impression; if you speak badly about one employer, you probably will do the same about others.

Succeeding in a Legal Job

Almost every attorney, paralegal, or other legal staffer will tell you (and if you are working in the field, you already know!): if you want to succeed at a legal job, it really helps if you like what you do. Almost any legal job will require a large time commitment, and most will involve a certain amount of drudgery. If despite those drawbacks you still find mental stimulation and personal satisfaction from the law, you will do well. If not, you may find yourself one of the many former legal workers who abandon the profession to seek greener pastures elsewhere.

The Billable Hour

The predominant method of collecting fees in private law firms is the by the hour. A law firm sets hourly rates for its various employees-partners, associates, paralegals, sometimes even secretaries—and then multiplies that hourly rate times hours worked to arrive at a price for legal services rendered. The more hours worked, the higher the bill. If you want to succeed at a law firm, you will probably have to bill a lot.

It is quite common for partners to cut hours on the bills they send to clients. Because the amount on the bill is calculated by multiplying hours times an agreed-on hourly rate, the only way to reduce the bill is to reduce the hours. If a partner decides that a bill

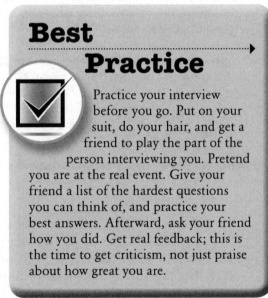

Best Practice

Practice your interview before you go. Put on your suit, do your hair, and get a friend to play the part of the person interviewing you. Pretend you are at the real event. Give your friend a list of the hardest questions you can think of, and practice your best answers. Afterward, ask your friend how you did. Get real feedback; this is the time to get criticism, not just praise about how great you are.

is too high, she may chop a few hours from an associate's or paralegal's billing. This may or may not hurt the associate's final tally; some firms make a distinction between billable hours recorded and actually billed, so cutting those hours could have a bad effect on the year's total. Nevertheless, best practices dictate that all attorneys and paralegals should still record everything they do.

INTERVIEW

What Does It Take to Make It in the Law?

Frank S. Holleman III
Attorney, Wyche, Burgess, Freeman & Parham

How long have you practiced law?
24 years.

What kind of law do you practice?
Litigation.

What tips for success would you give a young person just starting out in a legal career? What does it take to make it?
Consider your law degree as training in a way of thinking and analyzing problems. Look at options other than the traditional practice of law. Make sure that the path you choose fits your personality and your interests.

What are the most important qualities a person needs to succeed in the legal profession?
A successful attorney needs to be a good analyzer and writer, a problem solver, a person who can interact with and deal with a wide variety of people and organizations, and someone who puts the best interests of the client first. It is also important to have strong ethical values.

The longer you spend on a task, the more precise you need to be in your billing entries. If you spend eight hours reviewing a contract, your client will be happier to pay the full bill if it appears that those eight hours were all necessary. The hours will look more necessary if you provide a full description of what you did on the timesheet. Describing activities performed can be an art form, one that is not always taught in law school. Some firms have lists of codes that attorneys and paralegals use to describe what they have done. In other cases, you may need to compose your own phrases. The more specific you can be, the better. For example, if you spend two hours writing a letter, your bill will look better if it says "2 hours: write

I think an important point is to make sure that the career you choose fits your personality. Many people who go to law school are inclined towards the liberal arts and the social sciences. When they graduate from law school, many of the traditional career paths involve dealing with conflicts (litigation) or business. The recent graduate should consider whether the path s/he is choosing fits her/his temperament and interests.

How important do you think LSAT scores, grades (college and law school), and school name are for someone who wants to be a lawyer?
A graduate will have a wider range of choices entering the job market and thereafter if s/he is a graduate of a law school with a strong reputation. Attending a prestigious college and/or obtaining a strong LSAT score helps the student gain admission to the top law schools. Consequently, all these factors can be important and improve an attorney's odds of having a range of choices upon graduation from law school. At the same time, very successful attorneys graduate from every accredited law school in the country.

What do you think of the billable hour; is it essential for a lawyer to work insane hours in order to succeed?
It is reported that there is great pressure on new lawyers at many firms, particularly in large cities and in big firms everywhere, to bill certain numbers of hours. At the same time, there is a movement among lawyers and clients to find alternative means of billing that are not tied to the billable hour.

letter summarizing the topics covered during day's 8-hour deposition with former employee of chemical plant, including disposal of oil-filled paper capacitors, staffing of assembly line, and safety measures implemented during period 1958-1976 at facility in Pickens," than if it simply says: "2 hours: write letter."

The billable hour has for several years been widely criticized. Critics claim that it creates incentives for attorneys to work inefficiently, discourages creativity, fosters dishonesty in recording time, destroys collegiality because lawyers do not want to spend time talking with one another about non-billable matters, and is terrible for quality of life. So why is the billable hour still ubiquitous? Though no one seems to think billing by the hour is ideal, it is a simple way to generate fees for services and it seems to be the easiest way to set prices for complicated work. In addition, everyone is used to it. (For a good discussion of the drawbacks of the billable hour, see the ABA Commission on Billable Hours Report, 2001-2002.)

Despite the problems with the billable hour, it appears likely to stay around for some years to come. So how can you succeed in this area? The simplest method, if you are at a firm that emphasizes billable hours, is to work many hours and keep careful track of your time. If you find that this is too much, then the best option may be to find a job that doesn't emphasize billables so much. Some smaller firms do not require as many hours of their attorneys and paralegals. Corporations and government or public interest jobs often do not require billable hours at all.

Rainmaking

The most valued attorneys in any big firm are the lawyers who can bring in paying clients. These attorneys are known as rainmakers. Rainmakers find work in various ways, but generally they tend to be gregarious types who are involved in the community, especially the business community. Not every partner in a law firm is good at bringing in clients, but all of them are supposed to at least try. Most firms also expect associates to bring in clients if they can. All lawyers are encouraged to get involved in community activities, to serve on boards, and to attend events where they may meet potential clients. Firms spend substantial sums on entertaining existing clients—taking them out to lunch or dinner, paying for rounds of golf, and sending them gifts. If you end up working at a large or medium-sized firm, you will be encouraged to cultivate clients. If you work in a small firm or a solo practice, you will have to find clients if you want to make any money.

Unhappy Lawyers and Alternatives

It is no secret that many lawyers are unhappy with their work. Attorneys who work in firms are often the unhappiest. If you do become an attorney and find that law firm work is not for you (fear not, you will know!), remember there are alternatives.

For some attorneys, changing their status within the firm or moving to another firm can make a difference. Perhaps your firm will allow you to work part time. Perhaps you can get off the partnership track and work as a staff attorney, earning a reasonable salary for a reasonable amount of work. Another firm may have a culture and a practice that you find more amenable. Maybe you would like the freedom of working as a temp instead of being an employee. Perhaps you would really like to hang out a shingle and practice on your own.

Many attorneys find that moving from private practice into in-house or government positions is much more satisfying. These

Professional
Ethics

Hourly billing produces more than its share of ethical questions. For example, imagine you do a large amount of legal research for client A and bill client A for that time. The next week client B turns up with the exact same question; you have already answered it in client A's work, so you do not bill client B for the research. Client A has effectively subsidized client B, who benefits from the work you have already done for another client.

What about billing during travel? Say you are traveling on behalf of client A and choose to use the travel time to read documents for client B. Can you bill both clients for your time? No; legal ethics dictate that you can never "double bill," i.e. bill two separate clients for the same time. This is why some attorneys never work while they are flying. They see it as a waste of effort. It is permissible to bill for time spent flying, even if they sleep or read magazines the whole flight, and they do not get extra credit for working; if they bill by the hour, they will get more hours billed by doing the actual work after they arrive.

What about working late? Some attorneys bill for all the time they spend in the office after 5:00 P.M., even if they spend part of that time eating dinner and not working. Is this ethical? This apparently is something of a grey area. Attorneys who support this practice claim that they should be paid for staying late at the office, and that dinner is necessary to preserving their concentration. Opponents point out that billing for lunch is not ethical, and that clients themselves are not making attorneys stay late; working late is an attorney's own choice.

Problem
Solving

Finding the Right Fit

Thomas loved running a used bookstore, but after several years of near poverty, he decided that if he wanted to support a family, he would need to get a more lucrative job. He enrolled in law school. He loved the intellectual stimulation, the conversations with the professors, the law review, and working at a big firm in the summer. After graduation he clerked for a federal circuit court judge, the promise of a job at his old firm awaiting him the next year.

Alas, by the time Thomas finished his clerkship, that law firm no longer had a job for him. After several frantic phone calls to colleagues he found himself a job at another big firm in the same town. His salary was generous and the partners were kind, but Thomas found himself unhappy. There was the pressure to bill. There was the sense that he was not the firm's first choice. After four years, he decided he would never advance as he hoped to.

What to do? The happiest time in his legal career was his time in law school. He decided to go back to school to get an advanced degree in tax law. Another year of school got his head back in order and helped him find a job with the federal government, working on tax policy. The work is more like the intellectual challenge of law school, and the government hours are finite, unlike the law firm's. Thomas is content and looks forward to many more years in his position.

attorneys often have much more client contact, more control over the work they do, and saner hours. Getting away from the pressure to bill hours can be a huge relief.

Some attorneys take jobs in which they use their law degrees but do not practice law. Fields that can use lawyers include publishing, consulting, accounting, and teaching. Perhaps you would enjoy being a judge or magistrate, or working in alternative dispute resolution.

If you decide that the law really is not for you, you can quit and do something else. It may seem a shame to waste a law degree, but wasting your entire life in a career that makes you miserable is surely no better. This happens all the time; the Internet and libraries are full of resources on alternative careers for lawyers.

Hanging in There for the Long Haul

For attorneys who work in law firms, partnership is meant to be the ultimate goal. After all, partners are the ones who get to choose their work, delegate the boring parts to subordinates, and skim off the profits of the firm.

If you want to make partner, you should realize that you are in the legal profession for the long haul. It can take seven years or more of working as an associate to make partner. If you take time out to have a baby or two, it will probably take longer. Scores of associates drop out along the way, unhappy with the billable hour system, the work, or the fact that the practice of law does not measure up to their expectations. Not every associate who puts in the required years makes partner, either; some find themselves made into permanent associates, while a few find themselves fired.

Some attorneys stick with it, though. Those who do tend to be the ones who genuinely enjoy the practice of law. There can be a lot to enjoy. Legal work can present endless mental stimulation. Litigators talk about the excitement of arguing cases in court. Family law specialists find it very rewarding to resolve domestic difficulties, ensuring that parents and children have a stable existence. Corporate attorneys love the challenge of negotiating mergers between large corporations. Many attorneys have found great satisfaction in working at the same firm for many years, developing relationships with colleagues and nurturing younger lawyers.

If you know you want to be an attorney, do not be discouraged by statistics about declining numbers of jobs and general job dissatisfaction. There will always be work for those who are passionate about the law. If you really want to work in the legal profession, you have a good chance of finding a job that will keep you happy for the long haul.

Chapter 5

Talk Like a Pro

1L   A first-year law student. *2L*–A second-year law student. *3L*–A third-year law student.

401(k) plan   A retirement plan run by a company for its employees that allows employees to save or invest part of their salary tax-free and sometimes includes contributions by the employer.

accuse   To charge someone with a crime; to institute legal proceedings against a suspected criminal.

accused   Someone charged with a crime.

ACLU   American Civil Liberties Union, a national organization dedicated to protecting constitutionally guaranteed civil rights and liberties.

ADA   Americans with Disabilities Act, a federal law that prohibits discrimination against people with physical and mental disabilities.

ad hoc   Latin "for this"; arranged for one particular purpose. An "ad hoc committee" is a committee arranged for one specific purpose.

ad hominem   Latin "to the person"; appealing to the emotions instead of to logic and reason. An "ad hominem attack" is a personal attack on an individual's character, appearance, etc., as opposed to a logical attack.

adjudicate   To judge; to formally issue a final judgment in a court proceeding.

adjuster   A person who settles things, especially insurance matters; one who determines the amount of a claim against an insurer and then agrees on a settlement with the insured.

ad litem   Latin for "for the lawsuit"; for the purposes of the lawsuit being prosecuted. A guardian ad litem is someone appointed to act in a lawsuit on behalf of a child or incapacitated party.

administer   To manage; to run (a business or other operation); to give an oath; to enforce a decree. *administration*–the process of managing or running something; the people who manage something.

administrative agency   A governmental organization that implements a particular piece of legislation, such as workers compensation or tax law.

administrator   A person appointed by a court to handle the estate of someone who dies intestate, i.e. without a will. The feminine form is sometimes written administratrix. An "executor" is the person appointed to handle the estate of someone who dies leaving a will.

admissible   Acceptable; valid; able to be admitted. Admissible evidence is evidence that is proper to admit at trial because it is relevant to the matter at hand.

advance sheets   Recent judicial opinions published in pamphlet or loose-leaf form, which are later compiled into bound volumes of regional reporters, hardbound collections of court opinions.

adversary proceeding   A hearing or trial with opposing parties, one seeking relief from the other, and that ends with one party receiving a favorable outcome at the expense of the other.

advocacy   Pleading or arguing for a cause. Trial advocacy is arguing for a cause in court as part of a trial.

affirm   To confirm; state as fact; ratify; to declare that a previous judgment is correct. Affirmation is the act of confirming that something is true; affirmation can be used as a substitute for an oath in the case of religious or ethical objections to swearing.

affirmative action   Deliberate and positive efforts to help victims of discrimination by remedying effects of past discrimination and preventing future discrimination.

affirmative defense   In pleading, a response to a complaint that constitutes a defense and justification for defendant's actions instead of attacking the truth of plaintiff's allegations; affirmative defenses include self-defense, assumption of risk, estoppel, and insanity.

aforesaid   Said earlier; previously mentioned.

allege   To claim; to assert; to state in a pleading what one intends to prove at trial; allegation.

alternative dispute resolution   Methods for settling disputes without recourse to litigation, including arbitration, mediation, and conciliation.

ambulance chaser   A derogatory term for a lawyer who represents plaintiffs in personal injury cases.

amend   To fix; to improve; to modify or revise a document. An amendment is an addition of change formally added to a document, such as a constitution or contract.

amends   Reparations, something done to make up for a wrong done to someone else.

amicus curiae   Latin for "friend of the court"; someone who is not a party to a lawsuit but who has a strong interest in the subject matter of a case and petitions the court for permission to file a brief providing information on the matter to aid the court in rendering its decision; such a brief is called an amicus curiae brief or amicus brief.

appeal   To request a higher court to review a case that has been decided by a lower court and render a new decision, either a reversal or a new trial.

appeals court   A court that can hear appeals; also called a court of appeals or an appellate court.

appear   To come into court as a party to a lawsuit and submit to the court's jurisdiction. A party who appears in court makes an "appearance."

appellant   One who files an appeal.

appellate   Having to do with appeals.

appellate court   A court that reviews decisions made by lower courts and does not hear new cases.

appellee   The party against whom an appeal is filed; the party who prevailed at trial in the lower court.

arbitration   A form of dispute resolution in which a neutral third party renders a decision after both parties speak for themselves at a hearing.

arbitrator   A neutral person appointed or chosen to settle a dispute by hearing arguments from both parties and then rendering a decision at his or her own discretion, not bound by rules of law or equity.

argument   A set of reasons given in logical order intended to persuade hearers of a particular conclusion; a speech given by an attorney to the judge or jury in order to present a case and persuade the listeners to believe it.

arraign   In criminal law, to bring a defendant into court, charge him or her with an offense, and allow him or her to plead.

arraignment   The first step in the criminal process, in which a defendant is called into court, charged with a crime, informed of his or her rights, and allowed to plead guilty or not guilty.

attorney work-product   Materials prepared by an attorney or the attorney's employees in anticipation of litigation, which is protected from discovery by opposing counsel. In other words, opposing counsel cannot require an attorney to produce memos, reports, or briefs prepared as part of the attorney's preparation of a case.

award   To grant something; to give something as a prize or compensation; money or other object given as a grant or compensation; also the decision rendered by a non-judicial decider such as an arbitrator.

> # Everyone Knows
>
> The attorney work-product privilege is one of the more powerful types of privilege available to litigators. Among other things, it helps attorneys conceal their strategies from their opponents. The whole point of the privilege is to allow attorneys to work with some degree of privacy, free to assemble the facts they need without intrusion or interference by opponents.

bad faith   Deceit; intent to defraud; dishonesty in dealing with someone.

bail   Money or other security given temporarily to the court to allow a prisoner to be released before trial and to ensure that he or she will return for trial; if the prisoner does not return for trial, he or she forfeits the bail; to furnish money or property to get someone released from prison on bail.

bail bond   A contract between a prisoner, the state, and a third party known as a bail bondsman, in which the bail bondsman agrees to furnish bail for the prisoner in return for a fee and takes the risk that the prisoner will not return for trial.

bailiff   (1) A court officer who keeps order and looks after jurors and prisoners. (2) An agent or steward who is responsible for property or goods. *bailiwick*–a bailiff's jurisdiction.

bankruptcy   A process in which a court declares a person or business insolvent and orders the debtor's assets to be sold to pay off creditors, at which point the debtor is discharged from any further obligation and may begin anew. Chapter 7 bankruptcy is straight bankruptcy, a proceeding that liquidates property, pays off debts, and leaves the debtor discharged. Chapter 11 bankruptcy is business reorganization, in which a court supervises an insolvent business while it continues to operate and comes up with a plan for reorganization.

beneficiary   Someone who benefits from someone else's act, such as a person for whom property is held in trust, the recipient of the proceeds of an insurance policy, or someone named in a will as a recipient of property.

billable hour   A unit of time used as a basis for constructing bills for legal services.

boilerplate   Standardized text used in legal documents; text always written identically in the same kind of document.

breach   To break a promise; to fail to perform a duty or observe an agreement; *breach of contract*–Failure to perform acts promised in a contract; *breach of duty*–Failure to perform legal or moral duties, or to use the care that a reasonable person would use in given circumstances.

brief   (1) A written document presented to the court and to opposing counsel by a lawyer describing the facts of a case, questions of law, and legal arguments in support of his or her client's position. (2) A summary or abstract of a case. Can also be used as a verb meaning (a) To write a summary of a case, or (b) To inform someone of the details of something.

broker   A person who brings parties together to negotiate transactions between them in return for a commission or other compensation; a middleman; to negotiate a deal between parties; *real estate broker*–a person who negotiates transactions involving the buying and selling of land; *stockbroker*–a person employed by a customer to buy and sell securities on the customer's behalf.

call-back   A job interview at a law firm or other employer's offices, usually done after the employer has chosen a short list of candidates from on-campus interviews at a law school.

capital offense   An offense for which execution is a possible punishment; also called a capital crime.

capital punishment   The death penalty; punishment by death.

caption   The heading of a legal document such as a brief, motion, or pleading, containing the names of the parties, the court, and the action, the docket number, and any other required information.

case   (1) A legal action or lawsuit to be decided in a court or law or equity. (2) The legal arguments and evidence used by one side of a lawsuit to support its position.

casebook   A textbook used in law school to teach a particular type of law, containing court opinions from cases in that subject and commentary by experts in the field.

cause of action   A set of facts that creates a valid legal claim that can be grounds for a lawsuit.

caveat   Latin for "let him beware"; a warning.

caveat emptor   Latin for "let the buyer beware"; the principle that the buyer is responsible for examining merchandise and judging its quality before buying it.

challenge   To object; to dispute the truth of a statement; an objection.

chamber   A hall or room in which a judicial or legislative body meets.

chambers   A judge's private office.

citation   (1) A reference in a legal document or argument to a legal authority such as precedent or statute. (2) A summons issued by a court ordering its recipient to appear in court at a specified date and time.

civil action   A lawsuit brought by a private citizen to protect a private or civil right or to seek a civil remedy; a non-criminal action.

civil court   A court handling civil actions, i.e. non-criminal matters.

civil law   (1) Law concerned with citizens and private matters. (2) The body of jurisprudence created by a nation or state, as opposed to natural law or international law. (3) A system of jurisprudence practiced in Europe and in Louisiana, based on the codes of ancient Roman law as opposed to the precedents that form the authority of common law.

> ## Best Practice
>
> Most firms decide which candidates they will hire after call-backs. To enhance your chances of getting an offer, prepare beforehand—learn the names and practice areas of important attorneys—and be on your best behavior during the interviews. You may be taken to lunch or dinner; try to be a fun and gracious dining companion.

civil liberties Personal rights and immunities from government oppression established and guaranteed by the Constitution, including freedom of speech and freedom of association; natural liberties that cannot be limited by the government.

civil procedure The laws governing procedure and practice used in civil litigation.

civil rights The rights of all citizens to personal liberties, freedom, and equality. The difference between civil rights and civil liberties is that civil rights are specifically granted through laws enacted by communities. Civil liberties are not granted by law; instead they are natural rights that are inherent in all people.

class action A lawsuit brought by one or a few members of a group on behalf of all the members, specially certified by the court to confirm that all the members share a concern and meet other requirements.

clerk (1) A person who works in an office handling documents, records, and other administrative duties. (2) A court officer who keeps court records, files pleadings and motions, issues process, and enters judgment. A law clerk is a law student or recent law school graduate who assists an attorney or judge with research, writing of briefs, memoranda, and opinions, and other tasks. A clerkship is a period spent working as a law clerk.

client An individual or organization employing a professional to provide services; a person who employs an attorney to represent him or her in court, to draft legal documents, to advise, or to provide other legal services.

closing The conclusion of a sale of real estate, in which the buyer pays the purchase price, the mortgage is secured, and the seller hands over the deed to the buyer.

closing argument An attorney's final arguments to the judge and jury at the conclusion of his or her case, summing up the facts supporting the case and explaining why the opposing side's case is inadequate.

code A systematic collection of laws, regulations, or rules. Examples of codes include the civil code (code civil), which is the collection of laws based on the French Napoleonic Code that governs Louisiana jurisprudence, and penal codes, which are collections of laws dealing with criminal acts and punishments.

common law A system of law based on judicial precedent and custom rather than statute and code; the system of jurisprudence used in England and most of the United States.

community property   Property owned equally by husband and
wife, with all earnings divided equally between spouses; the form
of marital property distribution used by a minority of states.

company   A group or association of people with the purpose of
running a business or commercial enterprise; a business.

complaint   (1) The pleading that begins a civil lawsuit, in which
the plaintiff sets forth his or her causes of action and demands
relief. (2) In criminal law, a charge made before a magistrate
that a particular person has committed an offense, in an effort
to begin the process of prosecution.

conflict of interest   An ethical dilemma in which a person is
entrusted with two duties at odds with one another, in which
attention to one duty will harm the other.

conglomerate   A corporate entity composed of several different
corporations merged.

consideration   The payment or reward essential to the formation
of a contract and that persuades a person to enter the contract;
something of value given in exchange for a performance or a
promise.

construction   (1) The interpretation of a statute or legal authority,
particularly of ambiguous portions of it. "Strict construction"
is interpreting a statute solely on the basis of what is written,
bringing in nothing that is not expressed and looking for the
letter rather than the spirit of the law. "Liberal construction," on
the other hand, uses context, legislative intention, and other less
clearly specified methods to aid in interpretation. (2) Building
houses and other structures.

construe   To find the meaning in words or actions.

contingency fee   A fee charged by an attorney that is contingent
on a successful outcome of the case (commonly used by
attorneys representing plaintiffs in personal injury lawsuits).
Also called a contingent fee.

contract   An agreement between two or more parties that
is enforceable by law; a transaction between two or more
people in which one or both promise to perform some duty in
exchange for consideration and if a party fails to do what he or
she promised, the law allows the other party to seek a remedy.

contractor   A person who contracts to do work for someone else,
on an independent basis, using his or her own materials and
methods and not under the control of the customer with regard
to the details of how the work is done.

convict For a court to find someone guilty of a crime; a person who has been found by a court to be guilty of a crime.

conviction The legal act of finding someone guilty of a crime; the end of the prosecution, including the judgment or sentence.

copyright The legal right to publish, perform, or display a work of literature, art, music, drama, recording, or film, protected both by common law and by statute, including the Copyright Act of 1976.

coroner A public official who investigates sudden, violent, and suspicious deaths.

corporation The legal entity, created by law, of people who hold shares of a business, existing as a body that can sue and be sued but whose liability is generally limited to corporate assets.

correctional institution A jail, reformatory, prison, or other institution where those convicted of crimes are sent.

correctional system The government system of correctional institutions and parole systems.

corroborate To confirm or verify; to agree with or give support to.

court A tribunal in which a judge and/or jury hears and decides civil and/or criminal cases; the governmental entity that applies the state's laws to cases and controversies and administers justice; also called a court of law.

covenant A contract or formal agreement; often produced in writing and signed by all parties.

creditor A person or business to whom a debt is owed.

criminal One who commits a crime; one who violates a criminal law. Also used as an adjective meaning related to a crime; done with malice or intent to injure.

criminal justice system The government's system of law enforcement that apprehends, prosecutes, and punishes criminals, including law enforcement officers, courts, and correctional institutions.

criminal law The branch of law that deals with the prosecution and punishment of criminals; the body of law that determines what constitutes a crime and what constitutes suitable punishment.

cross-examination At trial or a deposition, the examination of a witness by the party opposed to the side that produced him or her, regarding testimony already raised on direct examination and matters of witness credibility.

custody (1) Responsibility or guardianship of a person or thing. (2) Imprisonment.

damages Money awarded as compensation for injury or loss.

debtor (1) A person who owes a debt to someone else. (2) A person subject to bankruptcy proceedings. *judgment debtor*–Someone who is the subject of a judgment awarding a sum to a creditor.

decedent Someone who has died.

decide To come to a conclusion or resolution after deliberation and consideration; to determine something.

decision A conclusion reached after considering facts and applicable law if necessary; a judicial determination or judgment.

decree The judicial decision of a court in equity made after hearing testimony and determining the rights of the parties, equivalent to a judgment by a court of law, though the term judgment may also be used in reference to courts of equity.

deed A written instrument, signed and delivered, by which one person conveys land to another.

de facto Latin for "in fact"; used to describe a situation that exists, through it might not be legal or official.

defendant The party against whom a lawsuit is brought; in civil cases, the party who responds to the complaint; in criminal cases, the person against whom charges are brought.

defense attorney An attorney who normally represents defendants in lawsuits.

defense firm A law firm that specializes in representing defendants in lawsuits, often paid by the hour.

de jure Latin meaning "by law, by right"; the condition of being in compliance with all applicable laws; legitimate and lawful.

deposition A form of discovery before trial in which an attorney questions a witness under oath and a court reporter makes a transcript of the testimony, which can then be used as evidence at trial.

discrimination Unequal or unfair treatment of people based on categories such as sex, race, religion, or age, when by all rights they should be treated fairly.

dismiss (1) To allow to leave or send away. (2) To terminate someone's employment. (3) For a judge to refuse to consider a lawsuit further, thereby ending it before a trial is completed.

dismissal A judge's order that terminates a lawsuit, motion, etc., without considering the issues involved in the matter.

district attorney A public officer of a state or county whose duty is to prosecute those accused of crimes within the area; different states use different titles, including prosecuting attorney, county attorney, state's attorney, or solicitor.

district court (1) A federal court that has jurisdiction over a particular region of a state and hears cases arising out of offenses against federal laws and cases involving litigants from different states. (2) In some states, an inferior court with general jurisdiction over minor matters.

docket (1) A list on a court calendar of cases scheduled to be tried. (2) On appeal, a formal record summarizing the proceedings of a lower court.

due process of law Fair judicial treatment guaranteed to every U.S. citizen by the Constitution in the Fifth and Fourteenth Amendments, which promise that no citizen will be deprived of life, liberty, or property without the opportunity to first defend him or herself, including the rights to a fair trial, to be present at one's trial, to be allowed to present testimony and to present evidence to counter the opposing side's case.

duress Conduct intended to force someone to do something he or she does not want to do, such as by threat of violence or coercion.

equal protection (of the laws) The principle that every person is entitled to the same treatment under the law as other people in similar conditions; equal *protection clause*–A clause in the 14th Amendment to the Constitution that prohibits states from denying people within their jurisdictions equal protection of the laws.

equity (1) A branch of jurisprudence that arose in England as an alternative to the harsh common law, in which courts tried to determine what would be fair in a given situation instead of strictly applying law and precedent, used in matters where the law was inadequate; today equity and the law have merged for the most part, but equitable principles and remedies still exist. (2) Fairness, justice. (3) The value of a property minus any mortgages or liens on it.

esq. An abbreviation for "esquire," often used to identify individuals who are licensed to practice law by having been admitted into a state bar. The correct usage is as a suffix, e.g. "Jane Doe, Esq."

evidence Anything used to prove the truth of an issue in court; includes testimony, documents, objects, and anything else that could persuade the jury.

fact finder   The person or group of people whose job is to determine the facts in a case; also called the trier of fact.

family court   A court with jurisdiction over matters related to families and children, including child abuse and neglect, support and custody, paternity, and juvenile delinquency.

federal courts   The courts of the United States, created by the Constitution or by act of Congress and having jurisdiction created by statute, including federal district courts, federal courts of appeal, and the Supreme Court of the United States.

Federal Rules of Civil Procedure   A compilation of rules created by the Supreme Court in 1938 that govern the procedure used in civil cases in U.S. district courts, and that have been used as a model for procedure by most state courts.

Federal Rules of Criminal Procedure   Procedural rules created by the Supreme Court in 1945 that govern proceedings in criminal cases before U.S. district courts and sometimes before U.S. magistrates.

Federal Rules of Evidence   Rules governing admission of evidence before U.S. district courts, U.S. magistrates, and bankruptcy court, and that have been used as a model for rules of evidence by many states.

felony   A serious crime; most felonies are defined by statute, and often include those that are punishable by death or by more than one year of imprisonment.

fiduciary   Involving trust, confidence, and good faith; describes the relationship of a trustee to a beneficiary or a guardian to a ward. Also refers to someone entrusted with a duty to act on behalf of and in the best interest of someone else, especially the management of someone else's property; a trustee.

finding   A court's or jury's conclusion about a matter of law or fact. A finding of fact is a court's or agency's determinations about the facts of a case after hearing testimony, examining evidence, and deliberating. A finding of law is a court's determination of how to apply law to the facts of a case.

forum   A court or tribunal; a place where people can try to get a judicial or administrative remedy for some wrong. "Forum shopping" is an attempt by a litigant to have the case tried in a specific jurisdiction that appears likely to rule in his or her favor.

fraud   Intentional misrepresentation of the truth to deceive someone into surrendering a legal right or otherwise being injured.

good faith   Sincerity, honesty, lack of deceit; a sincere intention to do what is promised.

grievance   A complaint; an allegation that someone has committed some injury or injustice that deserves recompense; in labor law, a complaint about working conditions filed by a worker or a union in order to seek relief.

guardian   A person who looks after the legal and financial affairs and/or takes care of someone who is unable to because of age or disability.

habeas corpus   Latin for "you have the body;" a writ that institutes a court proceeding to determine whether a criminal defendant has been lawfully imprisoned, or to test the constitutionality of a conviction; also used in cases of child custody and deportation.

headnote   A short summary of a case and its legal holdings placed at the beginning of the case report.

hearing   A legal proceeding, usually less formal than a trial, in which the parties to a case are given an opportunity to present evidence and testimony to a judge or other official who determines the facts and makes a decision based on the evidence presented.

hearsay   A report made by a witness of something that another person said or communicated nonverbally, usually not admissible as evidence.

heir   A person legally entitled to inherit an estate if its owner dies without a will; *heiress*–A female heir.

holding   (1) A court's ruling on an issue presented at trial; a legal principle produced by a court in deciding a case. (2) Property or stocks owned by someone.

hypothetical   Based on assumptions but not necessarily true.

hypothetical question   A question in which the questioner asks someone to offer an opinion based on the assumption that certain conditions are true.

inalienable   Not able to be taken away or given up without consent of the possessor. *inalienable rights*–Rights such as freedom of speech, equal protection of the laws, and due process that cannot be taken away from a person without his or her consent. An inalienable interest is a property interest that cannot be sold or transferred.

independent contractor   A person who does a job for another person independently, using his or her own methods and not under the control of the employer as to how the work is accomplished.

injunction   A court order prohibiting someone from doing a specified act in order to prevent future injury.

instrument   A formal written document; a writing that formally expresses some legal agreement, such as a contract, lease, will, deed, or bond.

insurance defense   Legal work done by a law firm that specializes in defending claims brought against or covered by an insurance company, usually with a special fee arrangement giving the insurance company discounted rates for high-volume work.

interrogatories   During discovery before trial, written questions about the case presented by one party to the opposing party that must be answered under oath and returned to the questioning party.

intestate   Without a valid will at the time of death.

JD   Abbreviation for juris doctor; the degree received by someone who completes law school.

John or Jane Doe   A generic name used to name a party to a lawsuit when that party prefers to remain anonymous. Sometimes the surname "Roe" is used instead of "Doe," as in *Roe v. Wade.*

judge-made law   A decision made by a judge that constitutes a legal precedent under common law; law that originates in judicial decisions rather than statutes; a judicial decision that contradicts the stated intention of a statute passed by the legislature.

judgment   The court's final decision in a trial; the amount of money awarded to the prevailing party by the court. A final judgment is a judgment that ends a legal controversy by conclusively stating whether or not the plaintiff is entitled to relief.

judicial   Related to the office of judge, judgments, the administration of justice, or courts; related to the interpretation and application of laws.

judicial authority   The power that comes as part of the office of judge; the power to hear cases and render decisions; also called judicial power.

judicial branch   The branch of government consisting of courts and other entities that exist to interpret and enforce laws.

judicial review (1) The power of the courts to review the acts of other branches of the government, usually in order to determine the law properly applied to a matter, especially in constitutional matters; review by the Supreme Court of acts by the legislature, as established in the case *Marbury v. Madison.* (2) Review of a trial court's decision by an appellate court.

jurisdiction (1) The power to make judicial decisions; a court's or judge's power to investigate the facts of a matter, apply law to them, and declare a judgment. (2) The territory in which a particular court can exercise its authority; the system of courts within a particular area.

jurisprudence (1) The philosophy or science of law. (2) The body of law formed by cases and interpretations of them; a system of law.

juror A member of a jury.

jury A group of people selected and sworn to hear the evidence in a case and decide what the true facts are, usually composed of a cross section of the community.

jury trial A trial that takes place before a jury, in which the jury hears the testimony and sees evidence and then renders a decision about the facts in accordance with the judge's instructions.

landmark decision A decision by the Supreme Court that changes the established law in an area.

larceny Taking the property of another person without the owner's consent and with the intention of keeping it.

last will and testament A will; the most recent will created by a deceased person; traditionally, the word "will" referred to the disposition of real property and the word "testament" to the disposition of personal property.

law review A professional journal published by a law school containing scholarly articles on legal topics by experts and students, usually compiled and edited by a staff of students chosen for their excellent academic record.

lawsuit An action at law or equity; a dispute brought before a court for determination.

lawyer An attorney; a person who has studied law or who practices law.

magistrate A public official with judicial, executive, or legislative power granted by the government, often functioning as a judge over minor matters or a justice of the peace. *Magistrate's court*–A court over which a magistrate presides, handling small claims and minor matters.

material Essential; important; relevant to establishing a cause of action or arriving at a judgment.

memorandum (1) An informal document that records the details of a transaction, event, or agreement, or discusses some matter. (2) A document that examines the facts of a case and applies the law to it to see whether it has merit or not, usually written by a law clerk or low-level attorney at the request of a higher-level attorney, and considered attorney work product; also called a memorandum of law or a memo.

moot court A mock court set up by a law school to try hypothetical cases as an exercise in oral advocacy for law students.

motion A formal application to the court asking for a rule or order in favor of the applicant, such as a grant of summary judgment, judgment notwithstanding the verdict, to dismiss a complaint, or a new trial.

municipal Related to a city or town or its government, or other local government; occasionally used in reference to state or national government.

n.b. Abbreviation of the Latin "nota bene," meaning "note well, observe"; used to draw a reader's attention to an important point.

natural law The body of law believed to be set by nature that applies everywhere and to everyone; for example, the belief that all people are created equal is said to be "self-evident," and not in need of any legal document to codify it.

negligence Failure to use the proper care in doing something, i.e. the amount of care that an ordinarily prudent person would use under the same circumstances.

notary public A person with the authority to perform a limited range of legal functions such as administering oaths, witnessing signatures, drawing up contracts or deeds, take depositions, etc.

oath The act of swearing that something is true; a promise to tell the truth in court or perform some act, often sworn before a witness or invoking a supreme power. The expression "under oath" describes an act done after swearing an oath.

oath of allegiance An oath binding the swearer to some nation or leader.

oath of office An oath sworn upon taking some office, promising to perform the office properly.

obstruction of justice Hindering the process of justice in court or of judicial acts, such as by influencing jurors or preventing an officer of the court from performing his or her duty.

of counsel Describes an attorney who assists in the preparation of a case but is not the lead attorney on it, or an attorney who is semi-retired from a firm or works at it part-time.

opening statement A speech made by an attorney at the start of the trial describing the facts and issues and arguments that the attorney will make.

opinion (1) A statement written by a judge explaining his or her decision in a case. (2) A statement written by an attorney for a client explaining his or her evaluation of the facts and law in a case. (3) Personal beliefs, views, or judgments on a matter.

oral Verbal; stated in speech, not in writing; *oral argument*–A verbal statement made by counsel before a court arguing in support of a position; *oral confession*–A verbal statement confessing to having committed a crime; *oral contract*–A contract that is made verbally, or partly verbally and partly in writing; *oral evidence*–Evidence provided through the speech of a witness.

order (1) A command or direction; a direction issued by a court to direct an action or determine a point of law. (2) A request or instruction to buy something or have something made. (3) The arrangement of several items or people in a sequence.

outline A summary of the key points of a document, argument, or topic, arranged as a list; a summary of the key points of a law school class done by a law student or a commercial publisher, created as a study aid. An outline group is a group of law students who collaborate on an outline for a class, such as by each contributing an outline of one week of class so as to compile a complete set of notes for the semester.

oyez A word meaning "hear ye," cried by a bailiff to mark the beginning of a court session; pronounced "oh yes."

pact An agreement between two or more parties.

parole The release of a convict from prison before the end of the sentence on the condition that the former prisoner follow certain rules and commit no more crimes. A parolee is a person released from prison on parole. A parole officer is an official who supervises parolees.

partner (1) A person who shares the profits and risks of some business or other enterprise with one or several other people. (2) A spouse or domestic partner.

party   (1) A person or entity involved in some transaction or matter; a person or entity on one side of a lawsuit or other dispute. (2) An organized political group that tries to make its own views the law of the land by participating in elections and working for common goals in government; also called a political party.

patent   (1) An exclusive right granted by the government to manufacture and sell an invention for a specified period of time. (2) A document granting land from a government to a person. (3) To obtain a patent for an invention.

perjury   The crime of intentionally lying under oath during a judicial proceeding, such as at trial.

personal injury   Physical injury to a person's body; also refers to a branch of law specializing in torts arising out of physical injuries.

personal injury lawyer   A lawyer who specializes in bringing lawsuits on behalf of plaintiffs who have suffered physical injuries.

plaintiff   A person who files a complaint to start a lawsuit.

plaintiff's attorney   An attorney who specializes in representing plaintiffs.

plaintiff's firm   A law firm that specializes in bringing lawsuits on behalf of plaintiffs, usually for a contingency fee.

plea   In criminal law, a defendant's response to the charges brought against him or her.

plea bargain   An agreement made between a criminal defendant and the prosecutor in which the defendant agrees to plead guilty to a lesser offense in exchange for a lighter punishment after conviction.

plead   (1) In criminal law, to answer charges brought by the prosecution. (2) To make or file a pleading in a lawsuit; to file a pleading in response to a plaintiff's complaint.

pleading   A document containing a party's side of a lawsuit, such as a plaintiff's complaint or a defendant's answer, in which the party lists the facts that support his or her side of the case and presents them to the court at the beginning of a lawsuit.

Ponzi scheme   A kind of pyramid scheme in which a perpetrator promises high returns on an investment and uses money submitted by later investors to pay off earlier investors, but eventually runs out of money or disappears and the scheme collapses.

power of attorney The authority to act for someone else in legal matters; a document conferring that authority to someone.

precedent A previously decided case that serves as a guide for deciding subsequent cases that have similar facts or legal questions.

prejudice Bias; prejudgment not based on actual experience or evidence; injury to a party that results from preconceived notions about the facts; to cause prejudice; to harm; prejudicial.

prima facie Latin for "first face," "at first sight"; based on first impressions; the initial view of something, accepted as true until disproven.

prima facie case An initial case; a case with sufficient proof to stand trial and withstand a motion to dismiss or for a directed verdict, and that will be accepted as true until the defendant proves otherwise.

prima facie evidence Evidence sufficient to establish a claim or defense until rebutted by contrary evidence.

privilege (1) A right, immunity, or advantage held by only one or a few people, or only by a particular group or class. (2) An exemption from duties or requirements imposed on most people; a release from an obligation or liability.

probate A formal court procedure in which a will is proven to be valid or invalid; the entire process of settling the estate of a deceased person.

probate court A court that handles wills, estates, and the appointment of guardians for orphaned children.

probation A sentencing procedure in which instead of imprisoning a person convicted of a crime, the court releases him or her to the supervision of a probation officer, with the understanding that a violation of the terms of probation will result in a prison sentence.

pro bono Latin meaning "for the sake of good"; describes work done for the public good, usually without compensation.

procedure A method of doing something; the formal steps and methods used in conducting a lawsuit.

proceeding A lawsuit or legal action; a step or event that is part of a lawsuit; a hearing, inquest, investigation, or other action that takes place before a judicial officer.

products liability A doctrine of tort law that holds manufacturers and sellers liable for injuries caused by defective products they introduce into the marketplace.

proof   The use of evidence or argument to establish a fact; evidence offered at trial to show the truth of some proposition.

pro se   Latin "for oneself"; appearing on one's own behalf; describes a person who represents himself or herself in a lawsuit.

prosecute   (1) To begin legal proceedings against someone, especially by the state against an accused criminal. (2) To continue to carry out some action intending to complete it; *prosecution*–The act of prosecuting; the party prosecuting a case; a criminal action; *prosecutor*–An attorney who prosecutes criminal cases on behalf of the state.

public defender   An attorney employed by the government to represent criminal defendants who cannot afford to pay for a lawyer.

public policy   The principles that guide a government in its administration, in an effort to maintain the well-being and order of the state and its citizens; also, the principle that a contract or transaction that harms the public good is illegal.

real estate   Land and the buildings attached to it.

rebut   To respond to an argument or claim with contrary arguments and evidence; to refute; *rebuttal*–The opportunity given to a defending party to respond to and refute the arguments presented by the party presenting a case in chief, or to the party who initiates closing argument after the other party has responded to that argument; an oral argument responding to and refuting an initial case.

record   An official written report about some event or transaction; written documents, audio and video tapes, and other documentary information.

sanction   (1) official approval of some action. (2) a penalty or threatened penalty for disobeying a law or rule; penalties taken by one nation against another, such as trade restrictions, intended to force it to comply with some standard.

security   (1) Safety; protection; the state of being protected from danger, loss, or threat. (2) Collateral; an item promised as a forfeit in case of default. (3) A stock, bond, debenture, or other interest that represents a share in ownership of a company or evidence of the company's indebtedness; an instrument that gives its owner the right to money or property.

seize   To take someone's property by force; for a police officer authorized by a search warrant to take the real or personal property of someone who has broken the law or who has been ordered to forfeit that property by the court; to take a person into physical custody.

sentence The punishment given by the court to a criminal defendant who has been found guilty of a crime.

separation of powers The division of the U.S. government and many state governments into three branches, executive, legislative, and judicial, each of which wields a particular set of powers unique to it and not shared by the other branches, and which the other branches are not permitted to use.

sequester (1) To isolate; to separate or segregate; to hide away; to isolate a jury during a trial. (2) To seize property pending the outcome of litigation or to hold until a debt is paid; to impose spending restrictions on a government; to declare someone bankrupt. Also called sequestrate.

serve (1) To work for someone, especially as an employee; to hold a position in the armed forces. (2) To deliver a legal document such as a summons formally and in an official capacity.

service The act of working for someone; the work that is performed by someone.

service of process The formal delivery to a defendant of the complaint, summons, or other legal document, to notify him or her that a lawsuit has been brought.

settle (1) To resolve a matter; to conclude an estate; to finalize accounts; for the parties to a lawsuit to resolve their dispute on their own before a court reaches a final judgment on the matter after trial, thereby allowing the trial to be cancelled and the lawsuit terminated. (2) To dispose of finally, such as after death; to give property to someone.

sexual harassment Employment discrimination that involves sexual demands and acts, that can involve perpetrators and victims of either sex.

small claims court A court that handles matters involving small amounts of money in an informal, inexpensive, and usually fairly quick manner.

solicitor (1) The head legal officer of a city, town, department, or other body. (2) (British) A lawyer who drafts wills, prepares conveyances, and handles all other legal matters aside from arguing cases in court, though in modern times solicitors do occasionally appear in court.

Solicitor General   The attorney who ranks just below the Attorney General of the United States and whose responsibilities include representing the U.S. government before the Supreme Court and other federal courts.

statute   A formal written law passed by a legislature.

statutory   Related to statutes; required by or governed by a statute.

subpoena   An official court document ordering a person to appear in court or at a judicial proceeding at a specified time.

summary judgment   A judgment that ends a lawsuit without trial in a case where a judge finds that there is no genuine issue of material fact and thus no need to send the matter to a jury.

summation   A last step in a jury trial before the jury begins deliberations, in which the attorneys for both sides sum up the evidence presented and call attention to the important points in their arguments; also called summing up.

summer associate   A law student who works at a law firm for the summer. Often called a clerk or law clerk.

suspect   A person who is believed to have committed a crime. Also used as a verb, meaning to believe without proof that someone has committed a crime or misdeed or to have some slight idea that something is the case without having any proof.

take the fifth   To invoke the Fifth Amendment as justification for refusing to answer a question in a criminal prosecution.

third party   A person who is not directly involved in a transaction; someone who is not a party to an agreement.

tort   A private injury or wrong; a violation of a socially recognized duty owed to a plaintiff that results in injury to the plaintiff; torts can be caused intentionally, through negligence, or under strict liability.

trademark   A name, word, symbol, or device registered with the U.S. Patent and Trademark Office and used by the manufacturer of a product to identify that product and distinguish it from other similar ones produced by competitors.

trial   A formal judicial proceeding in which a judge and sometimes a jury hear the evidence in a case and decide the rights of the parties in a civil case or the guilt or innocence of the defendant in a criminal case.

trial court   The court in which a case is first presented, as apposed to an appellate court.

tribunal A judicial court; a judge's seat or bench; a judge or group of judges with jurisdiction in an area.

Uniform Commercial Code (U.C.C.) A compilation of laws governing commercial transactions including the sale of goods, commercial paper, banking, and secured transactions.

Uniform System of Citation A guide to legal citation published by the Harvard Law Review Association and accepted as the standard guide to citation; also called the Blue Book.

United States Code (U.S.C.) A compilation of federal statutes, updated every six years and supplemented in between.

United States Code Annotated (U.S.C.A.) The annotated version of the U.S. Code, supplemented with case notes, cross references, and historical references.

vested Fixed; settled; secure in someone's possession; having the right to present or future enjoyment; established or protected by law or contract.

vested interest An interest that is recognized as belonging to someone who has the right to give it away; a personal stake in some matter.

warrant A written order issued by some authority directing someone to do a certain act, particularly an order issued by the state directing a law enforcement officer to arrest someone.

warranty A promise or assurance that something is true or that something is of a certain quality or useful for a particular purpose; an assurance by one party to a contract that a certain fact is true, given to save the other party the trouble of confirming it, that is in effect a promise to cover any losses suffered by the other party if the fact turns out not to be true; *warrantor*–A person who makes a warranty.

Chapter 6

Resources

Associations and Organizations

American Alliance of Paralegals This Web site for a national paralegal organization contains information on membership, certification, training, ethical standards for legal assistants, and more. This is a good place to find articles about the paralegal profession and its relationship to the legal profession as a whole. The Web site also has a job bank.   (http://www.aapipara.org)

American Bar Association The American Bar Association is an organization of more than 400,000 attorneys in the United States. If you are thinking about becoming a lawyer, you should visit the ABA Web site, which offers information on ABA-approved law schools, preparing for a legal education, succeeding in law school, getting admitted to state bars, and finding jobs. The site also has resources for professionals, including listings of continuing legal education opportunities, information on conferences, and articles on timely topics.   (http://www.abanet.org)

National Association of Legal Assistants This organization exists to promote the profession of legal assistant/paralegal and to establish professional standards. On the Web site, you can find information about working as a paralegal/legal assistant, follow current developments in the field, and search for training programs.   (http://www.nala.org)

Books and Periodicals

Acing Your First Year of Law School: The Ten Steps to Success You Won't Learn in Class. By Shana Connell Noyes and Henry S. Noyes (William S. Hein & Co., 2008). This book has been a bestseller since it was first published in 1999. It explains how law school works and gives students advice on how to allocate their time, especially during the anxiety-ridden first year.

American Lawyers. By Richard L. Abel (Oxford University Press, 1991). If you're interested in how the American legal profession got to where it is today, this is a good book to read. Abel traces the evolution of the practice of law over the past century, looking at lawyers' efforts to restrict access to their profession and to regulate themselves. He considers the many paths that law school graduates take, from private practice to business law to government work and even into judgeships or teaching.

The Firm. By John Grisham (Doubleday, 1991). This novel, published in 1991 and written by a lawyer from Oxford, Mississippi, spawned a new generation of legal thrillers. A Harvard law school graduate moves to Memphis to take a law firm job that seems too good to be true. Turns out it is—the firm is laundering money for the Mafia. John Grisham has since written a number of other legal novels that actually do show some of the reality of the legal profession. Remember you are reading fiction, though!

Getting to Maybe: How to Excel on Law School Exams. By Richard Michael Fischl and Jeremy Paul (Carolina Academic Press, 1999). Two law school professors explain how law school exams are put together, what professors are looking for in answers, and how to create those answers. Law school exams have stymied many previously successful students; any resource that can illuminate them can be helpful.

Law 101: Everything You Need to Know about the American Legal System. By Jay M. Feinman (Oxford University Press, 2006). This book, written by a law professor, covers the basic topics taught in the first year of law school: contracts, torts, civil procedure, property, and constitutional law. It is a good introduction to the American legal system and the way judges, juries, and lawyers work.

Law In America: A Short History. By Lawrence M. Friedman (Modern Library, 2004). A Stanford law professor describes the development of the U.S. legal system from a bare-bones descendant of English law to the current complex combination of civil and common law.

Law School Confidential: A Complete Guide to the Law School Experience. By Robert H. Miller (St. Martin's Griffin, 2004). This book is written by law students for prospective and current law students. It contains insider information about law school that will be useful for anyone considering acquiring a law degree. It discusses law school classes and grading, which schools grade pass-fail or on curves, how to work with a study group, tips for taking the LSAT, and much more.

Presumed Innocent. By Scott Turow (Farrar, Straus, Giroux, 1987). Practicing attorney Scott Turow wrote this book in 1987 and followed it with a number of other novels, all featuring litigator heroes. In *Presumed Innocent,* a former prosecutor finds himself accused of murdering the woman with whom he had an affair. The book contains lengthy scenes of the trial and cross-examination along with many lurid details of sex and murder. Turow also wrote a non-fiction book about his first year at Harvard Law School called *One L: The Turbulent True Story of a First Year at Harvard Law School.* (Grand Central Publishing, 1997).

> **Fast Facts**
>
> Other John Grisham novels include *The Pelican Brief* (1992), *The Client* (1993), *The Street Lawyer* (1998), and *The Associate* (2009). Grisham's first novel, *A Time to Kill* (1989), was inspired by an actual case he worked on involving a 12-year-old rape victim.

To Kill a Mockingbird. By Harper Lee (Harper Collins, 1960). Lee won the Pulitzer Prize for this novel, published in 1960. Scout, the young heroine, is the daughter of a small-town Alabama lawyer, Atticus Finch. She and her brother become embroiled in a drama of racial and class tensions when her father takes on the defense of a black man accused of raping a white woman. This is a great one for anyone who wants to get fired up about the law's power to fight injustice. Also check out the 1962 film starring Gregory Peck.

Other Media

Legally Blonde. For a treatment of law school with a large element of fantasy, check out this 2001 film (and its sequel, AND its live musical). Reese Witherspoon plays Elle Woods, a blonde sorority girl from California who decides to follow her ex-boyfriend to Harvard Law School. After some initial difficulty fitting in, Elle finds a way to thrive at Harvard on her own terms. Just do not imagine that this is what law school is really like!

The Paper Chase. This 1973 film stars Timothy Bottoms as a first-year student at Harvard Law School and John Houseman as the terrifying but brilliant Professor Charles Kingsfield. The Paper Chase is considered by many to be a classic depiction of law school, though it is certainly dated—for one thing, count the female and black faces among the law students. Watch it for fun but do not take it too seriously.

Web Sites

Above The Law This "legal tabloid" contains daily blog posts, articles, job advertisements, and other information for those who are currently working in the legal field. This is a great place to go to get a feel for the legal profession, as well as advice on acing interviews, job opportunities, and other timely topics. (http://abovethelaw.com)

American Society of Trial Consultants The ASTC is an organization of professionals who work with attorneys to enhance their effectiveness at trial. Members include experts in psychology, communication, graphic design, and theatre, as well as a number of attorneys. The Web site is full of articles on litigation and jury issues and publishes links to current stories about jury trials. (http://www.astcweb.org)

Animators at Law Visit this Web site to see what a company specializing in courtroom animations for litigation can do. (http://www.animators.com/aal/samples/samplesanimation.html)

CLEO (Council on Legal Education Opportunity) CLEO was founded in 1968 as a nonprofit organization to expand opportunities for low-income and minority students. With the goal of getting members of these groups into the legal profession, CLEO offers placement assistance, financial aid, academic counseling, bar exam prep classes, and many other resources to eligible minorities. (http://www.cleoscholars.com)

Electronic Discovery Law This blog, published by the e-Discovery Analysis and Technology Group at the law firm K&L Gates, keeps up with developments in e-discovery law and technology. (http://www.ediscoverylaw.com)

Findlaw This Web site has tons of information on the law for both professionals and the general public. You can go there to research bankruptcy, estate planning, how to deal with a DUI or DWI, starting a small business, health care, criminal justice, and other legal topics. Prospective clients can search for lawyers. If you want to try some do-it-yourself legal work, the Web site has a bank of legal forms available to fill out. Lawyers use the site for researching cases and statutes, showcasing their legal profiles, and advertising. Findlaw is owned by Thomson Reuters, which also owns Westlaw.   (http://www.findlaw.com)

Fast Facts

As of April 2009, Above the Law was chronicling major changes in the legal profession, including lower salaries, delayed starting dates for new associates, and fewer overall jobs.

Judicial Clerkships.com Interested in clerking for a judge? Visit this Web site, which contains links to Web sites related to finding clerkships. The forums are also interesting. If you want more information, you can order the Web site creator's book, *Behind the Bench:the Guide to Judicial Clerkships*, by Debra M. Strauss.   (http://www.judicialclerkships.com)

Law School Admission Council This is the organization that administers the Law School Admission Test, or LSAT. Their Web site has lots of information about the LSAT, including how to prepare, how to register, and how to get LSAT scores sent to law schools. It also has advice on choosing a law school, applying to law school, and legal careers.   (http://www.lasc.org)

Law Technology News This online publication follows the development of new technologies used in the legal field. It is a good resource for anyone who handles the technical side of the practice of law, including choice of hardware and software and security.   (http://www.lawtechnews.com/r5/home.asp)

LexisONE If you want to use LexisNexis' full research service, you must pay for it. If, however, you want to search for recent state and federal cases and don't need more research help than that, you can search for free at LexisONE. The Web site touts its "community," which includes downloadable forms, headlines, blogs and podcasts, and other content that doesn't compete with the company's other

Everyone Knows

"BigLaw" is a commonly used term that refers to the community of big law firms. To learn more or enhance your connection to this world, you can visit Law Shucks (http://www.lawshucks.com), a blog that chronicles life in and after BigLaw. In 2009, it was keeping an avid eye on law firm layoff trends.

services. (http://law.lexisnexis.com/webcenters/lexisone)

Monster Okay, this is definitely not a law-specific Web site. But if you are interested in legal work, you could do worse than to visit monster.com) from time to time to see what legal employers are looking for. The job advertisements here and on other Web sites (including Craigslist) can give you a good idea of exactly what jobs exist and help you decide where to focus your training. Monster ads also link to a number of law-specific employment agencies.   (http://www.monster.com)

NALP (National Association for Law Placement) NALP is a nonprofit educational association. It was founded in 1971 in order to assemble information in a way that would be useful to anyone involved in the legal field, from prospective law students to legal employers. Almost every ABA-accredited school and over 900 legal employers belong to NALP.   (http://www.nalp.com)

NALP Directory of Law Schools The *NALP Directory of Law Schools* is published annually in April or May. It contains up-to-date information of interest to recruiters, such as demographics, grading systems (important because not every school grades the same way), honors, and special programs and degrees. It also explains each school's recruitment procedures, providing schedules and contact information. It is available in print and online.   (http://www.nalplawschoolsonline.org)

NALP Directory of Legal Employers The *NALP Directory of Legal Employers* is published every year in mid-April. It contains information on more than 1,800 legal employers. The directory is available in print and online, but the online version is more reliable because it is updated throughout the year instead of just once a year. Job seekers can search for employers by geographic region, type of practice (public, private, etc), type of organization (such as corporations or government agencies), type of employees needed, billable hours, partnership policies, and more.   (http://www.nalpdirectory.com)

National Conference of Bar Examiners This is the organization that creates and administers the Multistate Bar Examination (MBE) and the Multistate Professional Responsibility Examination (MPRE). You can find study aids for those exams on the Wesb site as well as a comprehensive guide to bar admission requirements in all states and contact information for all state bars. This is also a good place to look for bar admission statistics. (http://www.ncbex.org/multistate-tests/mbe)

National Federation of Paralegal Associations The National Federation of Paralegal Associations, Inc., exists to promote "a global presence for the paralegal profession and leadership in the legal community." Like several other paralegal organizations, NFPA attempts to regulate standards within the paralegal profession. This Web site is the place to go to register for the PACE exam. Before taking the exam, you may want to purchase the study manual or take the seven-week PACE online review course. (http://www.paralegals.org)

NOLO Nolo's Web site is devoted to providing legal information, helping people take care of their legal needs, and connecting clients with lawyers. Nolo has been in the book publishing business for years, and still produces a number of titles every year on such practical topics as estate planning. It also publishes legal software, notably Quicken's WillMaker. On the Web site, you can find articles on such legal topics as handling foreclosure and bankruptcy and deciding whether to rent a house or apartment, or whether to create a will or a trust. You can also download legal forms such as stock wills, patent applications, living trusts, or incorporation documents.   (http://www.nolo.com)

The Order of the Coif This is the Web site for the legal honor society, the Order of the Coif. It contains a list of member schools, information on history of the organization, a schedule of a distinguished lecturer series, and more.   (http://www.orderofthecoif.org)

TrialSolutions This listing is not meant to serve as an endorsement for this particular business, but if you are interested in litigation technology, this Web site has some good examples of what is available. This company offers electronic discovery services and consulting, litigation support, online document review software, contract attorney staffing, and other support services.   (http://www.trialgraphic.com)

U.S. Courts This Web site explains the structure and operation of the federal court system. It has FAQs on how the federal court system works, how judges are selected, and how to file a lawsuit. It also lists job openings within the federal court system. (http://www.uscourts.gov/courtlinks)

Vault.com, Law School This Web site is a great place to go for current takes on law school and entering the legal profession. Find law school rankings, underrated law schools, advice on law school essays and taking the LSAT, and commentary on changes in the field. You can also read the results of student surveys from various law schools, which are useful for getting an idea of what the culture is like at a given institution. While you are at Vault, you can also research other types of careers in case you are undecided about whether law is right for you.   (http://www.vault.com/lawschool)

Index